PERSONAL EVANGELISM

Rup

PERSONAL EVANGELISM

By

J. C. MACAULAY, A.B., D.D.

and

ROBERT H. BELTON, Th.B., B.D., Th.M., D.D.

Instructors in Evangelism, Moody Bible Institute

MOODY PRESS

CHICAGO

Printed in the United States of America

Preface

WHEN I UNDERTOOK the preparation of a textbook in Personal Evangelism, I had sole responsibility for teaching this subject in the day school of Moody Bible Institute. It was recognized by the Administration that the class was too large, so after prayerful search a man was found to share the task. Dr. Robert Belton came from Kansas City, well equipped to assume this responsibility. I immediately felt that, if the teaching were to be shared, so should the preparation of the textbook. I asked Dr. Belton to collaborate with me in this undertaking, and he graciously consented to write Lessons 16 to 20, which deal with the particular types of cases met with in personal work. In a very real sense this is the heart of the book, and I am happy to have this part of the work executed by a man of such wide experience and gracious character.

Literature on the subject of evangelism is vast, and our temerity in adding to it can only be justified by what we hope is a freshness of approach and presentation. It is our earnest trust that others besides ourselves may find the work useful as an aid in presenting the great task of personal evangelism to eager young people. The form in which it is written should make it helpful to the general Christian reader who does not have the advantages of the classroom. Above all, may it bring honor to Him who alone is worthy!

—J. C. MACAULAY

Moody Bible Institute
March, 1956

Give Us a Watchword

Give us a watchword for the hour,
A thrilling word, a word of pow'r,
A battle cry, a flaming breath
That calls to conquest or to death.

A word to rouse the Church from rest,
To heed the Master's high behest.
The call is given: Ye hosts, arise,
Our watchword is, *evangelize!*

The glad evangel now proclaim,
Through all the earth, in Jesus' name;
This word is ringing through the skies:
Evangelize! Evangelize!

To dying men, a fallen race,
Make known the gift of Gospel grace;
The world that now in darkness lies,
Evangelize! Evangelize!

— OSWALD J. SMITH
Used by permission of the author

Contents

Acknowledgments

We are indebted to the following publishers and writers for permission to use the items indicated:

Dr. Oswald J. Smith, for the motto poem, "Give us a Watchword," page 6.

Mr. Norman P. Grubb, for checking the incident about Mr. Studd related in chapter 8.

The *Sunday School Times,* for the quotation from Mr. Norman Baker on page 23, and for the information about Mr. Gordon Forlong on page 117.

The Bethany Press (St. Louis 3, Mo.), for the quotation from Mr. Cartwright on page 21.

Hodder and Stoughton (London), for quotation from *Sister Eva of Friedenshort,* on page 241.

F. H. Revell Co. (Westwood, N.J.), for quotation from C. H. Spurgeon on page 69.

Moody Press, for incident concerning Dad Hall on page 54, and quotation from *The Life and Diary of David Brainerd,* page 74.

LESSON 1

What Is Evangelism?

SINCE PERSONAL EVANGELISM is a department of evangelism, our first inquiry must be in the more general field.

A. ETYMOLOGY OF WORD EVANGELISM.

The word comes from the Greek through the Latin. The Latin word is *evangelium,* derived from two Greek words— *eu,* meaning "well," and *aggelos* (pronounced *angelos*), meaning "messenger."

1. *Use of Word Aggelos.*

From the latter, as is quite apparent, we have our word *angel.* It is a common word in the New Testament, and its usages are varied and of great interest.

a) It is used of angels of God, heavenly beings of a high, spiritual order.[1]

b) It is used of fallen angels, heavenly beings who followed Satan in his rebellion, and who still oppose the kingdom and will of God.[2]

c) It is used of men, as John the Baptist,[3] John's messengers to Jesus,[4] those whom Jesus sent before Him on the way to Jerusalem,[5] the spies whom Rahab hid,[6] and the pastors

---

[1]Matt. 1:20; 4:11; Luke 2:9-15; Heb. 1:4-7, 13, 14.
[2]Matt. 25:41; I Cor. 6:3; II Peter 2:4; Jude 6.
[3]Matt. 11:10.
[4]Luke 7:24.
[5]Luke 9:52.
[6]James 2:25.

of churches.' This last is disputed by some, but the writer gives his opinion.

d) It is used of the spirits of men.[8]

e) It is used of the Lord Jesus.[9]

f) It is used of Paul's "thorn in the flesh," which he calls "the messenger of Satan."[10]

2. *Meaning of Word Messenger.*

A messenger is a bearer of a message. The message may be one of joy or of sorrow. That nature of the message does not affect the case. As a messenger, he is to give the message, good or bad.

But the Greeks were as eager for good tidings as anyone else, and they introduced the prefix *eu* to distinguish the bearing of a good message from the less pleasant duties of the messenger. Thus *euaggelidzo* meant "to bear a good message," "to tell glad tidings." By turning the *u* in *eu* into a *v*, as in the Latin *evangelium*, we have evangelize, the act of telling good news; evangelist, the one who bears good news; evangelism, the whole process of telling good news, and so on.

Very simply, then, our excursion into the etymology of the word tells us that evangelism is the telling of good news. As far as the word itself goes, it may be any kind of good news. In this primary sense, telling a student that he has earned an A grade, or telling a nervous young husband that his wife has been safely delivered of a son is evangelism.

Our word, however, has come to have a more specialized sense. We think of evangelism in terms of a specific body of good news, which we call *the* Gospel.

---

[7]Rev. 1:20.
[8]Acts 12:15.
[9]Rev. 8:3-5.
[10]II Cor. 12:7.

B. DEFINITION OF GOSPEL.

In the next lesson we shall study the content of the Gospel. For now, think of the wonderful meaning of the word itself. It comes down to us from the Anglo-Saxon *godspell,* which signifies *God's spell* (story), or *good spell.* The Gospel is God's good news for needy men. Evangelism, as we understand it, then, is the telling of God's good news, or the Gospel.

We must still more closely define our subject. The Gospel is a vast theme, and includes all that God does for men within the whole scheme of redemption. The story of how God saves sinners and brings them into right relation with Himself is Gospel. God's method of perfecting saints and at last presenting them "faultless before the presence of his glory with exceeding joy"[11] is Gospel. The message of the blessed hope is Gospel. How God turns our trials, toils, and temptations into "a far more exceeding and eternal weight of glory"[12] is Gospel.

C. SPECIFIC DEFINITION OF EVANGELISM.

According to our definition so far, the telling of any part of all this good news would be evangelism. However, we live in the days of specialization, and we generally restrict our use of the word *evangelism* to the telling of that portion of the Gospel which has particular reference to the unsaved. We go further. Not any kind of telling is evangelism. One might recite the Gospel in unbelief, in mockery, or as an academic diversion, and, while God might even use that to awaken and enlighten a needy soul, we could hardly call it evangelism. Here I should like to borrow a phrase from the

---

[11] Jude 24.
[12] II Cor. 4:17.

Roman Catholics. In the Roman Church grace is bestowed by means of the sacraments, but in order for the grace to be granted, the priest must administer the sacrament "with intention." This phrase, *with intention*, runs through much of the Roman system. We can use it here. That only is true evangelism which presents the good news of God "with intention." To state it specifically, evangelism is the telling of the Gospel to sinners with intent to bring them to a saving knowledge of Christ.

Evangelism is not everyone's job. It is the work only of those who have themselves been evangelized, and who have, by the grace of God, been joined to the company of the redeemed. The redeemed are a company, a Body, the Church. Evangelism is the work of the Church. When evangelism is carried on in complete detachment from the Body, it tends to degenerate into an unwholesome separatism. It is as members of the Body that we receive the life of the Head, and it is as members of the Body that we serve the Head.

So we arrive at our final definition. *Evangelism is the activity of the Church in telling the Gospel to sinners with intent to bring them to a saving knowledge of Christ.*

QUESTIONS AND EXERCISES

1. What is the etymology of the word *evangelism?*
2. In what senses is the word *aggelos* used in the New Testament? Give examples.
3. Give the simplest meaning of the word *evangelism*, derived from its etymology.
4. What is the derivation of the word *Gospel?*
5. Give a complete definition of *evangelism.*

The Message of Evangelism

GOOD NEWS is good in measure as it answers a bad situation. If I were a millionaire, and were told that a legacy of a thousand dollars had been left to me, I should probably smile an amused smile. But if I were six months behind in my rent, having no resources upon which to draw, and had just received eviction notice, the same piece of news would really be good news.

The Gospel is good news, because it answers a bad situation, and we cannot understand or appreciate the Gospel apart from the background of need which it meets. We must look, then, at the condition of man which called for God's saving intervention, and into which we must interject the good news.

A. MAN'S NEED OF SALVATION.

1. *The Guilt of Man.*

"All have sinned, and come short of the glory of God."[1] "There is none that doeth good, no, not one."[2] "There is not a just man upon earth, that doeth good, and sinneth not."[3]

Wrongdoing in man involves guilt, for man is a moral agent. Sins are not just mistakes. They are not a moral necessity. They are culpable infractions of the law of God,

---

[1]Rom. 3:23.
[2]Ps. 14:3.
[3]Eccles. 7:20.

13

and the stigma of guilt fastens upon every man for all his
sins.

2. *The Depravity of Man.* ~~Roman~~ I.

We cannot go into this as we would in a textbook of
theology, but a few Scriptures will make clear that we are
sinners, not only in the sense of having sinned, but also in
the sense of being sinful creatures, having a nature that
turns almost instinctively to evil.

Concerning the generation that lived immediately preceding the Flood, we read: "God saw that the wickedness
of man was great in the earth, and that every imagination of
the thoughts of his heart was only evil continually."[4] Our
Lord Himself has described the human heart: "For from
within, out of the heart of men, proceed evil thoughts, adul-
teries, fornications, murders, thefts, covetousness, wickedness, deceit, lasciviousness, an evil eye, blasphemy, pride,
foolishness."[5] That is not a pretty picture. The first chapter
of Romans contains such a description of the state of man
away from God that it is enough to make us tremble.[6] I
once heard a missionary tell how he had read this portion
of Scripture to a group in China. One Chinese rose up and
said in effect: "You are not reading that from your sacred
book. Someone has told you all about us in this village, and
you have come here to insult us by calling to mind all our
sins." The mirror of the Word was well polished that day!

This depravity of man does not mean that every man is as
bad as he can be, or that every man has committed all the
sins in the catalogue. It does mean that every man has this
sin nature in him, and that every man carries in his sin-bent
heart the seeds of all manner of sin. Of course, some are

---

[4]Gen. 6:5.
[5]Mark 7:21, 22.
[6]Rom. 1:21-32.

restrained by social custom, by religious training, by ethical principles, by gracious influences of one kind or another from engaging in the grosser acts, but no man can say that there is any act of sin which he is incapable of committing.

3. *The Alienation of Man.* James 4:4

As an outcome of the two foregoing conditions, man is alienated from God.

This alienation is two-sided. It arises out of the sinner's attitude to God, and God's attitude to the sinner.

a) Paul speaks of our unregenerate state as "when we were enemies,"[7] and describes us as "you, that were sometime alienated and enemies in your mind by wicked works"[8] James speaks of the world as the enemy of God, so that "whosoever . . . will be a friend of the world is the enemy of God,"[9] and that certainly includes all the unsaved.

It is true that men of the world often show a certain respect for God. They are moral men, who would not speak blasphemously of God. They will even mention God in public addresses and appeal to Him in the righteous causes which they have espoused. But this is respect at a distance. Let God draw near, and they will be uncomfortable. Let Him put His finger on their affairs, and their resentment and rebellion will quickly appear. So long as God "stays in His place" they will nod acknowledgment of Him, but let Him not touch their personal liberty!

b) The other side of the alienation is God's attitude to the sinner, so long as he abides in his sin. However men may reason, we cannot escape the awful reality of the wrath of God in the Bible. It is impossible for the infinitely

---

[7]Rom. 5:10.
[8]Col. 1:21.
[9]James 4:4.

holy God to be complacent in the presence of evil. He must express His utter abhorrence of it. The man in sin cannot stand before God. He is barred from His presence. He is under His wrath.

James Denny[10] has pointed out three expressions of the wrath of God as given in the New Testament.

(1) Three times in the first chapter of Romans the phrase occurs, "God gave them up."[11] This refers to a spiritual law, that when men deliberately choose evil, that evil is permitted to come to its full fruition. The operation of this law is an act of God, an expression of His wrath. Men who are given up to uncleanness, to shameful passions, to a reprobate mind are suffering the natural fruit of their own ways, but are in that also enduring the wrath of God.

(2) In the last verse of the same chapter, the apostle tells us that those who engage in such practices as he has listed in the previous verses know very well that they are wrong, and that God's judgment against them is death. This is the witness of the conscience to the wrath of God. Thus sinners carry around with them this sense of judgment. They are living consciously under the wrath of God. They may stifle it, and seek to suppress it by denial of God or by further plunging into evil, but it is still there.

(3) Finally there is "the wrath to come," the day of judgment, when men will be brought to final account, and the wrath of God will inflict the sentence of "everlasting destruction from the presence of the Lord"[12] on all who have continued in their sin.

4. *The Judgment of Man.* Rom 5 : 12

This has been touched on in Denny's third point regard-

---

[10]James Denny, *The Christian Doctrine of Reconciliation* (London: Hodder and Stoughton), p. 144.
[11]Rom. 1:24, 26, 28.
[12]II Thess. 1:9.

ing the wrath of God. It is sometimes forgotten that we belong to a condemned race. Adam was at first in a state of probation, until he sinned. We are not in a state of probation. "By one man sin entered into the world, and death by sin; and so death passed upon all men, for that all have sinned."[13] We are a race of sinners, condemned already. The judgment of the last day is not to determine where we shall spend eternity (on the basis of the balance between our good deeds and our bad deeds). That judgment is for universal demonstration of the righteousness of God, and for the carrying out of the sentence decreed. The righteous, the redeemed through faith in Jesus, will not come into judgment,[14] because of the great settlement made at Calvary.

5. *The Helplessness of Man.*

Not only is man in a state of guilt, but he can do nothing to cancel his guilt. Not only is he in a state of depravity, but he can do nothing to recover his unfallen nature. Not only is he in a state of alienation, but he can do nothing to effect reconciliation. Not only is he in a state of judgment, but he can do nothing to avert the judgment. If his desperate plight is ever to be alleviated, it must be through a sovereign, gracious act of God.[15]

B. GOD'S PROVISION FOR THE NEED.

Now the message of evangelism is that God has acted to reverse this fearful condition, that He has provided, and is now offering, a great and full and free salvation.

1. The fountain of this salvation is the love of God.[16] To some the love of God and the wrath of God may seem in-

---

[13]Rom. 5:12.
[14]John 5:24.
[15]Rom. 5:6, 16.
[16]John 3:16; Rom. 5:8.

compatible, but this is not so when we know the true nature
of both. The love of God is not soft sentimentalism, neither
is the wrath of God vindictive ire. The wrath of God may
be defined as the necessary reaction of holiness to all
moral evil, issuing in righteous judgment. His love moves
Him to deal with sin in such a manner that He can righteous-
ly forgive the sinner. Both His love and His wrath are holy,
pure, noble, and strong. They burn with the same intensity,
and are indeed part of each other. They could not exist
without each other. They are two expressions of the same
holy passion.

2. The Mediator of this salvation is the Son of God, our
Lord Jesus Christ.[17] He it was who became incarnate, and
as the God-man, wrought for God and man in the sacrifice
of Himself, thus obtaining eternal redemption.[18] He it is
who appears before the face of God for us, by whom alone
we draw nigh to God. God is our Saviour, but all the blessings of salvation are bestowed "through Jesus Christ our
Saviour."[19] There is no other way.

3. The content of this salvation is manifold. There is in
it an adequate answer to the entire lost condition of man.

a) *To Meet Our Gift There Is Forgiveness,*[20] *Cleansing,*[21]
and Justification.[22]

The forgiveness secures our restoration to the place of
favor; the cleansing takes away the defilement; and the
justification gives us a positive standing in righteousness
before Him. So our guilt is thoroughly dealt with.

b) *To Meet Our Depravity There Is Regeneration.*[23]

---

[17]I Tim. 2:5; Heb. 12:24; John 14:6; Acts 4:12.
[18]Heb. 9:12.
[19]Titus 3:5, 6.
[20]Eph. 4:32; Col. 2:13; I John 2:12; Acts 5:31; 13:38; 26:18.
[21]Isa. 1:18; I John 1:7; Rev. 7:14.
[22]Acts 13:39; Rom. 3:24; 8:30; Titus 3:7.
[23]John 3:6, 7; I Peter 1:22, 23; II Cor. 5:17; John 1:12, 13.

Regeneration means a new birth, from above, of God, making us new creatures, possessors of a new nature "which after God is created in righteousness and true holiness."[24] While this does not take away our old nature, it establishes an effectual counteraction to it. Then, since regeneration is accompanied by the indwelling of the Holy Spirit, we have the very power of God to render the old nature ineffectual and the new nature effectual. Thus our reason, our emotions, and our will are all delivered from the bondage of the depraved nature, and set free to serve God.

c) *To Meet Our Alienation There Is Reconciliation.*[25] *Rom. 5:10*

By the cross of Christ, God is placed in a new situation with regard to the sinner. He is now free to receive the sinner, not in his sin, but loosed from it. The sinner who will heed the exhortation, "Be ye reconciled to God,"[26] dropping his sword of rebellion and turning in penitence to the Saviour, will find the arms of God open to receive him into the full privileges of sonship.

d) *To Meet Our State of Judgment There Is the Gift of Eternal Life.*[27] *John 5:24*

Since the judgment is death, eternal life is its complete reversal. Being now "in Christ," the believer "shall not come into condemnation [judgment]; but is passed from death unto life."[28]

4. The divine method of salvation is threefold:
   a) *By Grace.*[29] *Eph. 2:8-9*

---

[24]Eph. 4:24.
[25]Col. 1:19-22; Eph. 2:13-18; Rom. 5:10, 11.
[26]II Cor. 5:20.
[27]John 3:14-16; 10:27, 28; I John 5:11, 12.
[28]John 5:24.
[29]Eph. 2:8, 9; Titus 2:11; 3:4-7; Rom. 3:24.

This makes it a sovereign act of God, altogether apart from human merit or works.

b) *By Blood.*[20] I Peter 1.18 -17

This signifies the sacrifice of Christ, His life given as an atonement for sin. Grace without blood would mean collapse of all moral values.

c) *By Faith.*[21] Rom 5'. 1

Faith is not a meritorious act which makes the sinner worthy of salvation, but a simple acceptance of the provided redemption. It involves repentance, for the very nature of salvation is such that an impenitent sinner cannot receive it.

QUESTIONS AND EXERCISES

1. List five aspects of man's condition calling for God's intervention in salvation.
2. State clearly the meaning of depravity as applied to the human race.
3. What are the two aspects of alienation as between man and God?
4. What are the three expressions of the wrath of God revealed in the New Testament? Give references
5. What particular state of man is met by (a) forgiveness? (b) regeneration? (c) reconciliation? (d) eternal life?
6. In three brief phrases describe God's method of salvation.

---

[20]Rom. 5:9; Rev. 1:5, 6; I Peter 1:18, 19.
[21]Rom. 5:1; John 20:31; Acts 20:21.

Criticisms and Character of Evangelism

Matthew 1:21

MANY HAVE BEEN THE CHARGES laid against evangelism. We are not surprised that the enemies of the Gospel should search out every weakness discoverable in the practice of evangelism and turn it into exaggerated accusations against evangelism itself. But many friends of the Gospel have been among the critics of evangelism, which fact makes it the more imperative that we take stock of ourselves and see wherein we may have given just cause for criticism.

A. SHORT IN ETHICAL VALUES.

One charge brought against evangelism is to the effect that it is short in ethical values. To put it bluntly, it does not produce real character in those who are won to Christ through its agency. Lin Cartwright has declared, with a degree of frankness: "This failure of the church to produce Christian character in the lives of those who have been reached by evangelism has wrought havoc with the morale of the whole Christian world."[1] If this is true, we face a serious indictment. But is it true?

1. *Emotionalism.*

That it is true of some evangelism, so-called, we shall have to admit. There is evangelism of a popular and hyper-

---

[1] Lin D. Cartwright, *Evangelism for Today* (St. Louis: The Bethany Press, © 1934), p. 13. Used by permission.

emotional type which almost hypnotizes people into "decisions," but gives them no sound basis of faith, leaving them to flounder in uncertainty for a time, and at last to return to "normal," which for them means the old life. The only change wrought in them is a determination not to be "caught" again. Their latter case is worse than their former.

2. *Entertainment*.

There is also a modern tendency to make evangelism very much a matter of entertainment. The sinner is lured to the evangelistic meeting for the "swell time" that is promised, and the devices of worldly amusement are unblushingly introduced. The appeal for decision heavily stresses the thrills of the Christian life. Very modern young people are put forward to testify that they are so happy, that being a Christian is one big thrill. Thus, in an atmosphere of entertainment, and with a one-sided picture of the Christian life presented, there is a great response. The sin question has been skillfully veiled, so naturally the young convert is not too much concerned with the ethical involvements of being a Christian.

3. *Believism*.

Yet again, too often a superficial view of "believing" is allowed to pass for saving faith. Many are ready to affirm that they believe in Jesus Christ when all they mean is that they are not Hindus, or Mohammedans, or Jews. They give mental assent to the Christian teaching. They have a historical belief, but no personal trust, no personal committal. Their belief has no accompaniment of repentance, no confession of Jesus as Lord. Yet on the strength of such a text as: "Believe on the Lord Jesus Christ and thou shalt be saved,"[2] they are encouraged to believe that they are

---

[2]Acts 16:31.

saved, and by virtue of their ability to quote the verse are received into the church. That is the heresy of "believism," and evangelism which operates on that basis will certainly not be fruitful in the realm of Christian character. Such evangelism may march under the banner of "the simple Gospel," but its protagonists ought to be reminded that there are no stronger "believers" than the devils,[3] although their belief cannot be called saving faith.

All this, however, is spurious evangelism, and true evangelism ought not to be held responsible for its counterfeits, any more than true currency can be blamed for phony dollar bills.

4. *Inadequate Follow-up Work.*

There is a great deal of true evangelism which is not brought to full fruition because of defects in the organization, or because of inability on the part of churches to follow up the work of evangelism with proper instruction and help.

Mr. Norman Baker, of London, reporting on Billy Graham's address at a gathering of 2400 ministers near the end of his great British crusade in 1954, quotes the evangelist as saying: "Of those helped at Harringay it is possible that 10,000 may not be adequately followed up because of lack of counselors and other immediate help."[4] There can be no doubt that the committee did an excellent piece of work in organizing the personal workers, but the crusade was just too big for their resources, and the results were beyond their computation. It may be, too, that the spiritual condition of the London churches had something to do with the inadequate supply of able counselors. Billy Sunday in his day was severely censured for leaving behind him

---

[3]James 2:19.
[4]*Sunday School Times* (Philadelphia), July 10, 1954, p. 574.

many converts who fell by the wayside, failing to manifest
any change of conduct. He would answer, "Put a newborn
baby in an icebox and see what happens!" Frequently the
failure to produce Christian character does not stem from
the evangelism, but from the lack of aftercare.

The beginning of our century witnessed the emergence
of what became known as the "new" evangelism. It pro-
posed to make up the deficit of the orthodox evangelism
by laying great stress on ethical values, character-building,
and the like. It had, however, a fatal weakness. It either
abandoned, or ignored, or minimized the atoning work of
Christ, which is the very heart of the Gospel. Such evangelism has an appeal to the cultured and refined, but without the cross it lacks what alone can produce Christian
character. This evangelism had no message for Skid Row
and the Bowery. It had no adequate answer to the cry of
the Philippian jailer, "What must I do to be saved?"[5] An
outstanding example of the new evangelism was Henry
Drummond. Himself one of the most gracious Christian
gentlemen ever to open his lips in Scotland, he nevertheless
represented a movement which proved completely inadequate. W. M. Clow, certainly no carping critic, wrote:
"A few years ago Henry Drummond, a forever endeared
name, himself a fully consenting believer, was preaching a
gospel which did not focus on the cross. His brilliant
gifts and his mesmeric personality gave his message a
potent charm. Crowds of young men flocked to his meetings. The movement has passed, and is little more than a
tender memory. The New Testament knows no Gospel
except that of the scorned evangelist."[6]

---

[5] Acts 16:30.
[6] W. M. Clow, *The Cross in Christian Experience*, p. 3.

The record is full and convincing. Evangelism, evangelical evangelism, the evangelism of the cross, works. It produces character, it maintains ethical values, it has no compromising with sin. "Thou shalt call his name Jesus, for he shall save his people from their sins."[7]

B. SHORT IN SOCIAL CONTENT.

While some charge evangelism with a lack of ethical content, others accuse it of having no social content. You are so intent on having souls saved, they say to us, that you have no interest in the welfare of the community. So evangelism stands pilloried as failing to affect society as a whole, or to touch the social disorders that abound. To meet this defect in traditional evangelism, the social gospel was propounded in the nineteenth century, gaining wide currency through the writings of Walter Rauschenbusch.

Now we shall frankly admit, or rather affirm, that evangelism is not social reform, nor does it aim directly at social reform. It is quite individualistic. It addresses itself to the individual, concerning his own life, his own conduct, his own salvation, his own relation with God, his own eternal destiny.

C. SOCIAL REFORM AND THE WORD OF GOD.

1. *Social Reform Implicit in the Gospel.*

But are there not social implications in all this? Does regeneration not affect all one's social relationships? If salvation does not make a man a better husband, a better father, a better workman, a better employer, a better citizen, a better neighbor, it is not salvation. What is social reform if it is not men treating each other better? Then let evangelism do its work, and you will have men scattered

---

[7]Matt. 1:21.

throughout society who are treating their fellows better, not because of some new legislation or some new social pattern, but because of a new spirit within them. These same men become a standard of conduct for those about them. Their conscience in a subtle way becomes the conscience of the group, and the group becomes dissatisfied with old conditions, catches glimpses of better ways, and moves out toward improvements. Even those who do not accept the Gospel become partakers of the benefits.

2. *Social Reform After Pentecost.*

The first great wave of evangelism in our Christian age was immediately followed by a social movement. The thousands who turned to Christ on the Day of Pentecost and after became at once aware of their social responsibility. "And all that believed were together, and had all things common; and sold their possessions and goods, and parted them to all men, as every man had need."* No one told them to do this. There was no social legislation. It was all perfectly voluntary and spontaneous, and while the method proved unsatisfactory for permanent adoption, the principle was established for all time. Evangelism, while not social in its method or emphasis, is definitely social in its results.

3. *Social Reform After Wesleyan Revival.*

The greatest era of social reform in all history followed, and grew out of, one of the greatest evangelistic movements of all history. The Wesleyan revival was a revival of evangelism. The Wesleys were primarily evangelists. But they recognized the social implications of the Gospel, and encouraged believers everywhere to fulfill their social obligations. This awakening was the fountain from which flowed a vast river of reform, affecting both Britain and

---

*Acts 2:44, 45.

America. Slavery, child-labor, unsanitary labor conditions, inhumane criminal laws, and many other abuses became matters of Christian conscience first, then of public conscience, and so of legislative action. The impact of the Wesleyan evangelism on all this has been indisputably presented by J. Wesley Bready in his two works, *England Before and After Wesley,*[9] and *This Freedom Whence?*[10]

4. *Social Reform Follows Missionary Efforts.*

It will scarcely be denied that the great evangelical missionary movements, while not social in emphasis, have been social in result. Age-long abuses, social practices of the most debasing type, have been brought to an end as an outcome of the preaching of the Gospel. Our missionaries have not simply said, "Be ye warmed and fed," but have built orphanages, leprosy colonies, hospitals, schools, and the like. Yet their evangelism has been of that individualistic kind which Peter and Philip and Paul and Silas practiced in the first century.

No doctrine, no system has been so reformative in its effects as the Gospel of Jesus Christ, simply because it is regenerative. It makes new men, and new men make new conditions. Communism is trying to establish new conditions without changing men, and it is using the instruments of hate, fear, murder, lying, oppressions, and force. It is bound to fail. In return for a few superficial changes, it robs men of freedom, of conscience, of personal rights. On the other hand, the Gospel makes new men who infuse into the social stream the elements of love, compassion, and personal responsibility. The process of social reform may seem slow to impatient souls, but we need only to look at

---

[9] J. Wesley Bready, *England Before and After Wesley* (London: Hodder & Stoughton).
[10] Bready, *This Freedom Whence?* (New York: American Tract Society). (Abridgment and a revision of his *England,* etc.).

our great freedoms, the honor accorded to womanhood, the care bestowed upon childhood, the provision made for the needy, our franchise, and compare these with lands where the Gospel is not known or has been rejected in favor of materialistic humanism, and we shall see how far we have come. We need no new Gospel, no new evangelism, but a mighty increase of sane, sound, Spirit-filled evangelism, and we shall witness its ethical and social values yet more abundantly.

QUESTIONS AND EXERCISES

1. What two charges have been brought against evangelism?
2. What tendencies in evangelism are apt to diminish the ethical quality of conversions?
3. What did W. M. Clow have to say about Henry Drummond's evangelism?
4. Who was the great proponent of the social gospel?
5. What evangelistic movement started a current of social reform which changed the face of history? Discuss.

Forms of Evangelism

EVANGELISM IS OPERATED in so many ways that it would be impossible to enumerate them all. We shall have to be content with a consideration of representative forms.

The forms of evangelism can be divided into two categories, having to do with the persons reached and the methods employed. Naturally there will be some overlapping.

A. PERSONS REACHED.

1. *Mass Evangelism.*

Here the emphasis is on gathering together as many people as possible in one place to hear the Gospel. There have been times when mass evangelism was in the ascendancy, and times when it has been in the doldrums. Such names as the Wesleys, Whitefield, Finney, and Moody are outstanding in the annals of modern mass evangelism. After Billy Sunday, however, this form of evangelism fell on evil days. It was freely declared that the days of mass evangelism were over. Prophetic teachers showed dispensational reasons for its passing, while others of a practical bent attributed it to the spirit of the age and advocated other forms and approaches to meet the changed atmosphere. There were, however, some die-hards who believed that the eclipse was only temporary, and that it only required new vision and faith and courage on the part of God's people to bring it back with greater effectiveness than ever. The die-hards

were right, and we have witnessed a resurgence of mass
evangelism which is unprecedented in all the history of the
church.

2. *Age-group Evangelism.*

Here the emphasis is on reaching those within particular age brackets. Special techniques are developed for
bringing the Gospel to young children, to teen-agers, or to
young people in general. This form of evangelism is represented by such movements as the Children's Special Service Mission of Great Britain,[1] the Canadian Sunday School
Mission, Child Evangelism Fellowship, Young Life Campaign, The Rural Bible Crusade, and Youth for Christ.
My first contact with age-group evangelism was the first-
mentioned of these, generally known as the C.S.S.M. The
missionaries of this organization were specially active at the
British seaside resorts in the summer. Here they mingled
with the youngsters who crowded the beaches, organized
sand-building contests, joined in the fun, made friends, and
held their happy services right on the sands.

I have just one criticism of age-group evangelism. It is
not inclusive enough. Why does it so much confine itself
to youth? There are other age-groups who need the Gospel. What about old people? They are the most neglected
of all. Few seem to care about their spiritual state. But
they are so hard to reach! And they have no life of service
to offer the Lord! Who said that we were to concentrate
on those who had a whole life to give? How long did the
thief on the cross have to live and serve the Master? Yet
our Lord, in the midst of His sufferings, took thought for
this dying criminal, and gave him the word of assurance.

---

[1]The mention of particular organizations is not intended to present them
as superiors to others in the same field, but simply as examples of the work
with which the writer is more familiar. We do not undertake to make
complete listings.

And are old people so hard to reach? What if they are? That gives us no excuse. They are not beyond reach. Gypsy Smith and his two newly converted brothers led their father and mother, aged seventy, to the Lord, and an uncle, aged ninety-nine![2] I personally have had the privilege of seeing the light break on aged faces, one a man of eighty-four. I should like to see "old-age evangelism," with special emphasis on kindness.

3. *Race-group Evangelism.*

Here effort is concentrated on reaching those of a particular race. In this field Jewish missions are a highly specialized activity, involving a religious as well as a racial situation. Indeed these two usually coexist. For instance, work among French Canadians involves a clash with Romanism; work with American Indians brings one up against the old tribal paganism; work with Chinese faces the obstacle of Confucianism or Buddhism. The whole genius of race-group evangelism is an understanding of racial psychology and religious background, and a sympathetic approach.

4. *Occupational-group Evangelism.*

Here the emphasis is on reaching those engaged in a particular occupation. Some occupations present a peculiar challenge, or a peculiar difficulty, or a peculiar opportunity. These call for action. For instance, men going out to the mines or forests of Canada lived in company "shanties," rather crude dormitories, separated from their families and from home comforts for considerable periods, such as the logging season. They were exposed to much temptation, and had the long evenings on their hands. Some Christian men caught the vision, and the Shantymen's Christian Association was formed to minister to these men.

---

[2]Gypsy Smith, *Gypsy Smith, His Life and Work* (London: Law), p. 58.

The missionaries of this association are hardy men (a few women too!), prepared for hardship and sacrifice. Our home in Sault Ste Marie, Canada, used to be a stopping-off place for some of them on their way to and from their fields, and we knew something of the rugged life involved. But those rough workers out in the bush knew that someone cared, and many have been won to the Lord.

For many years there has been excellent work carried on among the policemen and railwaymen of Britain, on the principle of infiltration. Every Christian policeman or railwayman was expected to be an "agent," and provision was made for their fellowship and group witnessing. The last time I visited the Tent Hall in Glasgow (one of the largest missions in the country), I shared the program with a team of Christian policemen from Belfast, Northern Ireland. They were an enthusiastic group.

Work among servicemen is not new. Chaplains have long been a recognized part of the military forces of many countries, but in addition to this official provision, soldiers' and sailors' and airmen's Christian associations, homes and service centers have developed in many parts of the world.

The Inter-Varsity Christian Fellowship should be included here, since it is concerned, not so much with an age-group as such, but with an occupational-group, men and women temporarily occupied as students in institutions of higher learning. In this case there is a certain uniformity of age involved, and the fact that men and women are within reach of this particular testimony for such a limited time gives the greater urgency and concentration to the work of the Fellowship.

The Inter-Varsity Fellowship was born in England, and operated there for some time before it spread to Canada, and thence to the United States. In recent years it has grown rapidly, till now it is active on more than seven hundred campuses in this country alone.[3] The work is now international in scope, being carried on in many parts of Europe, Asia, Australia, South Africa, and Latin America. While there is no over-all world direction, the various national groups have a common bond in the International Fellowship of Evangelical Students (IFES).

5. *Special-need Evangelism.*

In this case attention is focused on those who are in straits of divers sorts. The rescue mission is an outstanding example. Here human derelicts are welcomed, their immediate physical needs cared for, and the Gospel presented by men and women who understand. It is difficult work, and often thankless work, but the recompense is great in seeing "broken earthenware" remade by the regenerating and sanctifying power of the Holy Spirit. The Salvation Army has performed distinguished service in this sphere, a good account of which is given in Harold Begbie's *Twice-Born Men.*[4] The Pacific Garden Mission of Chicago, the Water Street Mission of New York, and the Mel Trotter Mission of Grand Rapids, Michigan, are notable representatives of hundreds of such efforts to "rescue the perishing."

Jails, hospitals and other institutions offer special fields of evangelism. Burdens of guilt, sickness, poverty and age call for sympathetic and careful dealing.

6. *Personal Evangelism—Individual Work.*

Here the emphasis is on reaching the individual. H. Clay Trumbull's motto was, "Individual work for individuals." In the long run, every other form we have mentioned reduces itself to this. Whatever the characteristic of the

---

[3]The *U. S. A. Directory* for June 30, 1954 gives the number as 708, including regular chapters and informal groups, in universities, colleges, and schools of nursing.

[4]Harold Begbie, *Twice-Born Men* (Westwood, N. J.: Revell).

group with whom we are working, our aim is to win the individual. We are not after the crowd but the persons who make up the crowd. We are not interested in the student as such, the railwayman as such, the youth as such, the derelict as such, but we are seeking the person who happens to be a student, a railwayman, a youth, or a derelict. They are all lost. They are all precious. Christ died for them all. We see them all as souls, as persons. As such we must seek them.

B. METHODS EMPLOYED.

1. *Public Meetings.*

This is the method which naturally answers to mass evangelism, and which has been used throughout the Gospel age. There is something inspiring and convincing about a great crowd of people. While we must never put our confidence in mass psychology for saving results, we shall not forget that it does have a part to play. Is it not an ordinance of God, which can indeed be perverted to evil uses, but can also be used for God and by God? When a sinner is brought into a large Gospel gathering where there is wholesome enthusiasm, he cannot but be stirred. His complacency will be jolted, his self-assurance shaken. He may resist, but he will not be the same. He has been exposed to the Gospel. He has been where God was present and working through His Word.

When this form of evangelism is employed, every effort should be put forth to make it count. An evangelistic meeting without sinners is like a wedding without bride and groom. On the other hand, an evangelistic meeting that is not well supported by the saints will give any sinner who does happen in a poor impression of the urgency of salvation. True, God can work in very small gatherings, as he did that stormy day when He saved young Spurgeon

in a Primitive Methodist chapel, but ordinarily God works
with His people, and when they are stirred to action and
bring sinners to the hearing of the Gospel, results are to
be expected.

2. Radio. *impersonal*

Here is a twentieth-century development which has become one of the most effective instruments for propagating the Gospel. Today great networks carry the mes-
age. The pioneer of network Gospel broadcasting is
Charles E. Fuller, who began broadcasting over a single
station in January, 1926, but now sends the "Old Fashioned
Revival Hour" over more than six hundred stations, with an
estimated audience of ten million.[5] Add to this Billy Graham's "Hour of Decision," now utilizing two national networks, the Lutheran Hour, the "Back to God" broadcast of
the Christian Reformed Church, and you see how the
Gospel is receiving an unprecedented hearing. There are
stations wholly devoted to the work of the Gospel, such as
WMBI of Chicago; HCJB of Quito, Ecuador; ELWA of
Liberia, West Africa; DZAS of Manila; TIFC of San Jose,
Costa Rica; and TGNA of Guatemala City. Thus the mission fields of the world, including the closed regions, are
being penetrated with the message by radio. It is an amazing phenomenon.

But it is not easy. Radio evangelism calls for special
skills and techniques. In the public meeting the preacher
has the advantage of personal presence. His whole personality comes into play. He can sense the attitude of his
audience and act accordingly. In radio he loses all of his
personality except what he can put into his voice, and he
cannot change tactics to answer audience reaction—not
until the letters begin coming in! The man whose voice

---

[5]*Moody Monthly* (Chicago 10), January, 1955, p. 21.

lacks personality is greatly handicapped in radio, and people are not required to "sit through" the sermon. Think of the successful broadcasters. They have personality in their voice. To take only two already mentioned: Charles E. Fuller's voice is tender, caressing, and persuasive, while Billy Graham's is dynamic and commanding.

3. *Television.*

This form of evangelism, like television itself, is just in its infancy, but it is bound to grow. It is expensive, but that will level off. There is tremendous potential here for evangelism. However, while it is generally classed with radio, its chief difficulty is in the opposite direction. We noted that in radio there is a loss of personality which must be compensated for in the voice. In television the whole personality is restored, but is now exposed to more critical scrutiny than ever it was in the pulpit. Men who have done well in radio, because of a personable voice, may find themselves playing a meager role in television because of a general personality which does not fit the screen. My wife and I used to listen to a commercial program on the radio. The announcer had a pleasing, cultured voice which made even his routine advertising not at all distasteful. One day we visited friends who had television, and this same program came on. We never wanted to hear it again. The personality of the announcer was insipid and rather effeminate. The appeal was gone. So once again, new skills, new techniques must be developed for television. Awkward passes that would be little noticed in the pulpit, and not seen at all in radio, will shout from the housetops in television.

4. *Literature.*

This will include Bibles, Bible portions, tracts, magazines, and books. With literacy increasing at a tremendous rate in formerly backward parts of the earth, this instrument of evangelism needs to be cultivated much more rapidly. Too often we have allowed false cults to beat us to the draw in this field. Not only the increased literacy of Africa and Asia, but the revival of religious interest in our own land calls for a greatly accelerated program of literature production and distribution.

a) The Wycliffe Translators and the Bible societies are doing a herculean work in preparing the Scriptures in the tongues of the peoples of the world. And many agencies, such as the Gideons, the Pocket Testament League, and the Scripture Gift Mission, are widely distributing the Scriptures—whole Bibles and portions.

b) The Gospel tract has been greatly improved in recent years, especially since Mr. Clyde Dennis caught the vision of applying modern techniques of printing in this field. Before that, most Gospel tracts were so cheap and unattractive that it was an embarrassment to use them. There is still room for improvement, however, in the material. There are some excellent tracts, but many very poor ones. Frequently the approach is repulsive, or there is a lack of challenge, or the English is poor, or the language is foreign to those whom we wish to reach, or it fails to make the point. We need Gospel writers of ability, writers who not only have truth and zeal and grace, but who think clearly and write clearly.

c) When it comes to larger works, we have a terrible scarcity of material of worth beamed for the unsaved. One of the phenomena of our age is the frequency with which religious books break into the best-seller class, and these set the pattern for the faith of multitudes. But how often is this true of a soundly evangelical work, whether fiction or non-fiction? Billy Graham's book, *Peace with God*,[6] made the grade, but in addition to its own excellence, behind it was the tremendous publicity of his great campaigns and his radio network program. Here is a wide-open field for men of daring and imagination and faith, who are at the same time men of letters.

For one thing we can be thankful. The Bible itself is a best seller. It still goes out in the millions each year, and we have the divine promise that "it shall not return unto me void."[7]

d) A new development in this sphere is the correspondence course. The correspondence course itself is not new, but has been largely confined to the instruction of Christians. The new feature is in using it as an instrument of evangelism. The need and the demand called it into being. The purpose is to present the elements of the Christian faith so clearly and simply that the unsaved, untaught in the Bible, will be led step by step into the knowledge of the Way. One of the clearest statements of the way of salvation I have ever read, in regular correspondence form, with questions attached to each lesson is *The Good News*. The Correspondence School of Moody Bible Institute has this course.

5. *Phonograph Records.*

We were not first in this. Jehovah's Witnesses had it before us. Apart from records of Gospel music, this method of evangelism has not taken much hold in the English-speaking world, but it is developing rapidly as a tool of missionary endeavor. *Gospel Recordings* of Los Angeles pioneered in this field, and today are distributing records in a thousand languages and dialects.[8]

---

[6]Billy Graham, *Peace with God* (Westwood, N. J.: Revell).
[7]Isa. 55:11.
[8]Moody Monthly (Chicago 10), March, 1955, p. 87.

6. *The House-party.*

The Oxford Group Movement specialized in this method, but it has worked well in evangelical circles also. It is a distinctly European plan. Mr. Tom Rees, of England, has had remarkable success with it. A few years ago I shared in the ministry at his conference center, Hildenborough Hall, with a group of about a hundred and fifty young people. It was not a camp, but a house-party. The house was a magnificent manor with spacious grounds. While the guests were not expected to dress formally for dinner, Mr. and Mrs. Rees did, and it added a touch of English culture to the scene. Recreation was, of course, provided, such as riding, tennis and the like, while there were afternoon excursions by bus to Canterbury and London for those who desired to explore the regions beyond. But everything centered on the spiritual aim. Classes were held, and there were periods of counseling, the quiet time, and hours of happy fellowship. It was not easy for an unsaved person to go through a week of this without yielding to the Lord, although there was great care not to bring undue pressure on any. Perhaps we could explore this method more than we have done.

7. *The Bible Camp.*

This is definitely an American feature. Concentration of effort is joined to the relaxation of camp life. The free-and-easy atmosphere tends to break down barriers and induce frank discussion. As in the house-party, the Bible camp presents a real challenge to the leaders and to the Christians attending, for unless the living corresponds to the teaching, the effect on the non-Christian can be disastrous. There must be many hundreds of conversions among American young people each summer as a result of the scores of camps conducted in every section of the country. I could wish that statistics were available.

8. *The Movie.*

This is another twentieth-century invention which has been pressed into the service of the Gospel. Christian movies fall in two categories—the documentary and the dramatic. In the former, there is no acting, in the technical sense. In the latter, acting is the chief medium.

a) There is little prejudice with regard to the documentary film. The Gospel science films of the Moody Institute of Science, for instance, are generally accepted, and are being used in many countries, having been translated into fourteen languages. They are also used in the armed services, in schools, in factories, and have access where other Gospel agencies are unacceptable. Their usefulness as instruments of evangelism is beyond dispute.

b) When it comes to the dramatic movie, however, there is a sharp division of opinion. As I write, I have before me an article[9] by Walter Smyth, who heads up the Billy Graham Evangelistic Films, Inc. Naturally he is all out for the dramatic movie as an evangelistic weapon, and points to the more than one third of a million recorded decisions resulting from the showings of Billy Graham's films, both documentary and dramatic.

On the other hand, many Christian leaders are not impressed with these figures. They suspect that decisions made under the impact of such highly emotional appeals may in the end have a deleterious effect on the church as a whole. Over against the policy of using every available means, we have the other philosophy that we shall be safer to abide by Biblical methods, in reliance upon the Holy Spirit. Take this from A. W. Tozer,[10] in an address

---

[9]*The King's Business* (Los Angeles), December, 1954, p. 26.
[10]*Moody Monthly* (Chicago 10), January, 1955, p. 17.

given at the Mid-America Keswick Conference in October, 1954: "Again, there must be a return to New Testament methods. Some people say, 'We believe in the Bible message, but we believe in modern methods.' My brethren, the church is busy today, certain sectors of it, preaching a Bible message and then canceling out all of the good they do with the methods they use to promote that message. We must go to the Bible for our methods as well as our message."

No doubt experience will teach us whether the effects of the religious dramatic movie are natural or spiritual, temporary or permanent; whether the Holy Spirit is using it, or whether it is a substitute for the Holy Spirit; whether it is a divine provision for our day, or whether we are trying to do spiritual work with carnal means. Not the immediate response, but the ultimate effect upon the church, will be the test.

9. *The Bible Class.*

We are not now thinking of the Bible classes which constitute the adult department of a Sunday school. The evangelistic note should not be absent from these. But what we have in mind is a spontaneous movement which has come into being in late years. It is very quiet and unobtrusive, and is better to be kept so. Moreover, it is completely informal. In a certain community there is a Christian home surrounded by non-Christian homes. The Christians are friendly and neighborly, and have a burden for their neighbors. One evening they invite half a dozen couples in, and give them a pleasant time, while at the same time keeping control of the conversation. After a while such topics as the world situation, the new religious interest, men's need of God, and a national turning back to the Bible are discussed. An interest is manifest. The Christians (or perhaps some of the non-Christians!) propose getting together to study the Bible. Is there anyone who would be our teacher and guide our discussions? Of course the host and hostess know someone! Generally it is better that that someone be not a preacher. A time is set, and the informal but guided studies begin. The unfolding of the great plan of God begins to grip. Some may drop out, but others come, invited by members of the class. After a while some of these socialites are beginning to speak Christian language, and wonderful confessions of faith are made. That is actually taking place in many towns and cities, usually in the "better" communities.

In such situations it is important to maintain the element of personal friendship, to avoid "meeting" techniques, and to bar sectarian discussions. The teacher does not lecture, but guides, explains, helps.

10. *Personal Evangelism—Methods Employed.*

We included this under forms with respect to persons reached. We now consider it as a method employed. Finally all evangelism is personal. The Holy Spirit deals with individuals, and all our methods must be aimed at the individual. If the singling out of the individual is the divine method, it must ultimately be ours. One man face to face with one man in an encounter for God—you cannot imagine a more dramatic, a more powerful situation. That is Personal Evangelism. The accidents surrounding that situation may be of infinite variety, but there is the unvarying essence of it—one man face to face with one man in an encounter for God. That is the theme of the rest of our study.

QUESTIONS AND EXERCISES

1. Into what two categories can the various forms of evangelism be divided?

2. List all the forms of evangelism you can think of with respect to persons reached, not confining yourself to those dealt with in the textbook.

3. As a research project discover the outstanding names in mass evangelism in the past three centuries (two or three for each century), and write a brief description of the work of each. You are not necessarily confined to the English-speaking world.

4. Write brief accounts of some group-evangelism undertakings with which you are personally acquainted.

5. Compare radio and television evangelism, and indicate the benefits and problems of each.

6. Compare the house-party and the camp as methods of evangelism.

7. Discuss the pros and cons of the movie as an instrument of evangelism.

LESSON 5

The Place of Personal Evangelism

IN HIS VERY HELPFUL WORK, *The Effective Evangelist,* Fletcher makes this statement: "From my own experience I am compelled to admit that preaching to crowds must be followed by conversation with individuals, for it is in coming into touch with individuals that the most important work is done. Some people may be stirred in a big meeting; but rarely does a man come into the light until he is led there by individual instruction. The getting of a crowd, then, is only a means to an end—that end being the coming into touch afterward with individuals; and that can be done also in other ways, even if the crowd is never gathered."[1]

An examination of this statement shows that personal evangelism can be used in two ways—in conjunction with other forms of evangelism, and quite independently of other forms. Fletcher insists that the gathering of a crowd is in order to separate needy individuals and have them individually dealt with, and then suggests that this separating of individuals for personal dealing can be done without the gathering of a crowd. In this lesson we shall look at personal evangelism from these two angles.

A. IN CONJUNCTION WITH OTHER FORMS.

It is frequently stated that Peter's sermon on the Day of Pentecost resulted in the salvation of three thousand. This

---

[1] Lionel B. Fletcher, *The Effective Evangelist,* p. 167.

44

is true, but it does not tell all the truth. We must remember that Peter had the support of one hundred and twenty who were giving their own witness.[2] There can be no doubt that they became mingled with the multitude and that the preaching was reinforced by many a personal conversation. We are not told of any deliberate organization of the one hundred and twenty, and, indeed, in that situation such organization would have been out of the question. Nevertheless, Pentecost set the pattern for all later evangelism, namely, the preaching supported by the personal work.

1. *Supplementing the Evangelistic Campaign.*

Today the best evangelists insist on a trained corps of personal workers. Experience has shown that where this is lacking the final results of an evangelistic crusade are greatly weakened. In the large meetings of the Chapman-Alexander Team, the training of the personal workers was a major part of the entire effort. Much care was taken in screening applicants, and the whole program of personal dealing was supervised, none being allowed to take part in the work unless he could show his identification badge. It is a matter of public knowledge that the preparation of the counselors for Billy Graham's campaigns begins long before the arrival of the evangelist on the scene.

I have known evangelists who insisted on doing all the personal work themselves. In such cases they were engaged in smaller campaigns in individual churches which could not provide men and women capable of this delicate work, and in desperation the evangelist undertook to do it himself. This, of course, lays a terrible burden on the evangelist, and few could stand up to it for long. But whether done by himself or others a true evangelist insists on personal work.

---

[2]Acts 2:4-8.

2. Supplementing Radio Evangelism.

The more impersonal the form of evangelism engaged in, the more imperative is it to open channels for personal dealing. There surely can be no more impersonal form of evangelism than radio. Some way must be found to compensate for this. I remember speaking to a good friend of mine who had long experience in radio work, concerning my difficulty in broadcasting from a studio. That little piece of metal into which I spoke gave me no inspiration. My friend wisely did not tell me to think of the multitudes who were listening, but he said, "Think of one person, perhaps an old woman seated by her radio in some little cottage out in the country, or of a traveler riding along in his car with his radio tuned in, and talk to that one person." That was good advice. If it is followed there will be a personal note in this most impersonal form of ministry.

Good radio ministers also encourage correspondence from their hearers, not just for financial support for their broadcasts, but so as to follow up their long-distance ministry with more personal contacts. It is evident, of course, that the radio preacher himself cannot visit all who write to him. In such a case it is good for him to be in touch with evangelical pastors throughout his radio field so that he can pass on to them such correspondence as calls for personal contact. In this way he not only secures for the inquirer the needed help, but puts him into the care of a local church. On several occasions, when I was a pastor in Wheaton, Illinois, a radio station director passed to me such responsibility, and the results were usually very gratifying.

3. Supplementing Bible Camp.

As another example of the value of personal work in conjunction with other forms of evangelism, we can think of its vital blessing in the Bible camp. However effective the other ministries of such a camp may be, the director and his helpers lean very heavily upon the personal touch. The primary duty of the counselors is to watch the young people to see what impressions are being made, and prayerfully to step in with that personal instruction and encouragement at the supreme moment.

It is not too much to say that whatever form of evangelism is being engaged in, personal work is not only a helpful but a necessary supplement.

B. INDEPENDENT OF OTHER FORMS.

Philip was an evangelist—a successful evangelist. He was engaged in one of the most thrilling campaigns of his whole life when the Spirit of God told him to leave Samaria, the scene of his fruitful labors, and go off into the desert to meet one man.[*] So we find Philip transferred from a pulpit, with great multitudes listening to his preaching, to a carriage, with a foreigner for an audience. Not all men could adjust themselves to such a change, but Philip was as successful in personal evangelism as he was in mass evangelism, with the result that this foreigner, the personal treasurer of the queen of Ethiopia, returned to his own land a rejoicing, and no doubt, a witnessing Christian.

We have seen that the preacher, Peter, had the support of one hundred and twenty personal witnesses, but there is no indication that the Ethiopian had to attend a public service to have the work finished which Philip began. It will be generally agreed that personal evangelism is more self-contained than other forms of evangelism, and does not need their support as much as they need its support. Perhaps that is even an understatement. At any rate it is a form of evangelism in its own right.

---

[*]Acts 8:26-39.

Personal Evangelism can be carried on in a variety of ways.

1. *Unplanned (Occasional) Personal Evangelism.*

By this I do not mean simply personal evangelism once in a while, but rather as the occasion arises. A good example of this is the "chance" meeting on a train. I shall not say that a commuter train offers the most inviting opportunity for personal witnessing. My experience has been that most people are so engrossed in their newspaper, or so completely drowsy, that conversation is the exception rather than the rule. Even then, however, an alert Christian will get in a word here and there. Longer journeys invite conversation, if for no other reason than to escape boredom, and then a Christian has his opportunity, especially if he has prayerfully prepared his own heart.

On one occasion I was traveling from Buffalo to Cleveland. Occupying a vacant seat at Buffalo, I quietly prayed that the Lord would bring someone to sit with me to whom I might be able to witness. A young man came and sat beside me. As soon as he spoke I knew he was an Irishman, and I presume that as soon as I spoke he knew I was a Scot. Conversation was easy, and before long we settled down to talk about spiritual matters. I learned that his parents were Christians and that he was on his way to Cleveland for a family reunion. He did not yield to the Lord, but when he knew that I had a church in Cleveland he affirmed that he would bring the whole gang to hear me preach the following Sunday evening. I hoped for the best. The Sunday evening service opened with no sign of my Irish friend, and as the minutes passed without his putting in an appearance, I decided that it had been just another one of those insincere promises. However, as we sang the hymn immediately preceding the sermon, about a dozen people marched in, led by my young friend. The one to whom I spoke on the train has not to my knowledge accepted Christ to this day, but one of his brothers continued to attend the church and some weeks later came to me at the close of a service and said, "Pastor, I want to accept your invitation to come to Christ." He became a radiant Christian, trained for Christian Service, and went as a missionary to Africa where he has now given several terms of very fruitful service.

There are some lessons for us in this incident:

We must keep our hearts prepared.

We must not give up easily.   *go between*

The one to whom we first talk may be a *liaison* to the one whom we shall win for Christ.

Such occasional witness is not, of course, confined to the train. As we go about day by day we must be on the lookout for opportunities.

2. *Planned Personal Evangelism.*

This can be in co-operation with the program of a local church. During a campaign of visitation on unchurched people in Wheaton my wife called on a woman of considerable means and culture. Conversation discovered that years previously she had had some contact with another woman who was now an active Christian in the church. My wife, believing that the best strategy in this case was to bring these two together again, reported the case to this Christian woman, who immediately invited her former friend to her home. Now in this home a Bible class was conducted of such a nature as we described in the lesson on forms of evangelism. The worldly woman became interested, attended the Bible class, and after much searching opened her heart to the Saviour. She is now with the Lord, and her husband, who had shown no interest, later sought the way of salvation.

There are other definite plans besides the house-to-house visitation program. A Christian man in an office or factory has a mission field all prepared for him. He can prayerfully set his sights for one individual after another, and having sought guidance from the Holy Spirit, follow the leading given him in an effort to win his fellow workers one by one. It was by such means that William Carey was won to Christ—through the consistent and persistent testimony of a fellow apprentice, William Warr.[4]

I believe many Christian men fail in this opportune situation by trying to witness to all in a general way instead of concentrating on one at a time. A definite plan, prayerfully laid, would be much more effective than dependence on the chance opportunity.

BASIC SUGGESTIONS FOR EVANGELIZING.

1. *Use Common Sense.*

Should we evangelize everyone we meet? The answer will have to begin with definitions. What do we mean by *meet*, and what do we mean by *evangelize?* It is quite evident that if we were walking down State Street, Chicago, or Fifth Avenue, New York, it would be a physical impossibility to present to every individual whom we met on those busy thoroughfares a personal and complete statement of the Gospel. One must decide, therefore, what type of meeting lays on him a responsibility for witness, and he will also have to distinguish between the obligation to give a passing word of testimony, and the requirement to undertake a more complete presentation of the truth.

---

[4]F. D. Walker, *William Carey* (Chicago 10: Moody Press), pp. 31, 32.

2. Be Ethical.

The ethical question may enter into our personal evangelism. For instance, we have no right to rob our employer of the time which we have contracted to work for him. If two men are working side by side on a more or less mechanical job permitting conversation without interference with the work, then the Christian may witness to the non-Christian in such a situation, but where such personal dealing requires a cessation of work another time will have to be chosen.

3. Avoid Embarrassment.

Witnessing in a situation which would cause embarrassment to the party witnessed to is unwise and likely to be unfruitful.

4. Know When to Desist.

Insistence on pressing the subject of salvation where it is quite evident that the party in question does not wish to speak about such matters is likely to make the sinner more determined to have nothing to do with the Gospel.

5. Buy Up Opportunities.

With all this in mind, one should nevertheless regard all with whom he has sufficient contact to make personal dealing possible a potential hearer of the Gospel, and seek guidance from the Holy Spirit in opening conversation. H. Clay Trumbull, the author of *Individual Work for Individuals*,[5] set it down as a principle to be followed, that when the direction of a conversation was in his control he would turn it to the things of God.

6. Obey the Holy Spirit.

We must learn to be obedient both to the urgings and

---

[5]H. Clay Trumbull, *Individual Work for Individuals* (New York: Association Press), p. 23.

the restraints of the Holy Spirit, just as Paul obeyed the restraint of the Spirit with regard to preaching in Asia and Bithynia,[6] but obeyed the urge to witness in the synagogues and market places of Athens.[7]

7. Be Prepared.

The final answer is personal preparedness, with wisdom and judgment given from the Holy Spirit.

QUESTIONS AND EXERCISES

1. In what two ways can personal evangelism be practiced?
2. How was Peter's sermon on the Day of Pentecost supported?
3. What part does personal evangelism play in such campaigns as those of Billy Graham?
4. Discuss the statement: "The more impersonal the form of evangelism engaged in, the more imperative is it to open channels for personal dealing." Give examples.
5. Give an account of a successful evangelist in the New Testament who turned to personal work.
6. What do we not mean, and what do we mean, by unplanned (*occasional*) personal evangelism? Give an example from your own experience.
7. Discuss the question, "Should We Evangelize Everybody We Meet?"

---

[6] Acts 16:7-10.
[7] Acts 17:16.

LESSON 6

The Advantages of Personal Evangelism

HOW FAR WOULD YOU AGREE with the following statement by H. Clay Trumbull: "As a rule, the intensity of the appeal is in inverse proportion to the area covered; in other words, the greater your audience, the smaller the probability of your appeal coming home to a single heart"?[1]

If we really believed that, we should not be so anxious to build big churches, but should rather seek to limit their size by increasing their number. But even those who would be inclined to accuse Mr. Trumbull of overstatement here will readily admit the truth which he is trying to press home, that personal evangelism is finally the most effective of all. Its advantages are many. Some of them we shall now examine.

A. ALL CAN DO IT.

By all, of course, we mean all Christians. Now I do not know of any other form of evangelism of which this can be said. Not all can preach, not all can write, not all can sing, not all can act, not all can organize a camp, not all can teach a class, but all, irrespective of age, sex, or ability, can do personal work.

This does not mean that all will be equally skillful or equally successful. We cannot deny that some are special-

---

[1] H. Clay Trumbull, *Individual Work for Individuals* (New York: Association Press), p. 3.

ly gifted for this type of work. Very few could match Uncle
John Vassar, for instance. As a personal soul-winner he
belongs to an elect circle. Some indeed have affirmed that
all we need is enough prayer and enough faithfulness and
the fullness of the Holy Spirit to make any one of us equal
to the best. But that is forgetting the sovereignty of the
Holy Spirit in distributing the gifts.[2] God put His Holy
Spirit upon Bezaleel[3] for the making of the furnishings of
the tabernacle, but that does not mean that if he had been
faithful enough and prayerful enough he could have been
as great a leader as Moses—no more than prayer and faithfulness could have made Moses an artist in gold and silver
and brass and wood. We must acknowledge the special
endowments of the Spirit as well as the enduement of the
Spirit.

Still we repeat: here is one work which all can do, each
in his own measure, and no doubt more prayer and more
faithfulness would make us all abler and more effective.
Many have been used of God in this sphere despite serious
handicaps. Indeed the handicaps of some have determined
the form of their service. "Dad Hall,"[4] affectionately known
as the "Bishop of Wall Street," inaugurated the now international telephone ministry at the age of seventy-five, when
he was just recovering from a stroke which paralyzed his
left side. A "wrong" number started it all, resulting in
fifteen calls that day, and it kept increasing till three tele-
phones and several helpers were kept busy.

My eldest sister, now with the Lord, was invalided with
a heart ailment for years. She used to read the society
columns in the newspaper. One day she was taken with
a sense of responsibility for those of whom she was read-

---

[2]I Cor. 12:11.
[3]Exod. 31:1-5.
[4]Sara C. Palmer, *Dad Hall* (Chicago 10: Moody Press), p. 116.

ing. After much prayer, she began to write letters to them —gracious letters of congratulation or condolence, as the situation required, and always a witness for Christ. The effectiveness of her humble ministry was apparent in some of the replies.

B. OPPORTUNITIES ABOUND.

That certainly is not true of other forms of evangelism. Many would seek in vain for an opportunity to fill a pulpit, to appear on television, to speak on the radio, or have a book published, but we are daily surrounded with opportunities to witness for Christ. Our difficulty is failure to recognize them, or if we recognize them, to seize them. If we are thoroughly truthful, we may have to admit that sometimes we try not to see them.

It is written of Adoniram Judson that "every social relation was a tie by which men might be drawn heavenward."[5]

In the first chapter of John's Gospel, three different social relationships are seen as spheres of witness—discipleship, kinship, and friendship. John the Baptist told his disciples,[6] Andrew told his brother,[7] and Philip told his friend.[8] The home, the office, the factory, the school, the place of recreation, all become spheres of witness to the soul-winner.

C. IT FOCUSES ATTENTION ON THE INDIVIDUAL.

Psychologists tell us that there is something of the herd instinct in us all. But there is something else too. We are all very conscious of ourselves as individuals, and we like

---

[5] Edward Judson, *The Life of Adoniram Judson* (New York: Anson Randolph & Co.), p. 311.
[6] John 1:35-37.
[7] John 1:40-42.
[8] John 1:45, 46.

attention, not merely as members of the herd, but as individuals. Even those who seem to shrink most from attention crave it. We know how the "not wanted" feeling has driven many to despair and self-destruction.

The fact is, we are a bundle of contradictions. Our ladies, for instance, want to be in style and dress according to the present fashion, yet if they see another wearing a dress the same as theirs, that dress will be quickly discarded. There must be both conformity and distinction! So everyone wants to be like the rest of the fellows, and yet feel that he is different. Each man is a special case in his own eyes. And he is, too! God has made him so. For all the broad and fundamental likenesses there are no two exactly alike. If it is so in the snowflakes, it is more so among men endowed with the precious gift of personality.

We are all alike in the fact of sinnerhood and our need of salvation, and the same salvation is applicable and adequate to every man's need, but the individual complexities of every man's nature will determine the manner of his coming to God. Now the more general forms of evangelism may reach a man as a member of the herd, but personal evangelism will touch that sense of solitariness. The voice of the preacher may tell him that "God so loved the world, that he gave his only begotten Son,"[9] but if someone cares enough to approach him personally, it will be easier for him to believe that "the Son of God . . . loved *me*, and gave himself for *me*."[10] The personal worker may be the living demonstration of what the sinner longs to know, that "the Lord thinketh upon *me*."[11]

---

[9]John 3:16.
[10]Gal. 2:20.
[11]Ps. 40:17.

D. IT ENABLES ONE TO DEAL WITH INDIVIDUAL PROBLEMS.

Perhaps this is the reason why some of us shrink from coming to grips with the individual. We are afraid we may be asked questions that we cannot answer, and face problems for which we have no solution. In a public address *we* bring up the questions—those to which we have the answer, or think we have. But in personal work the other party poses the questions, and how devastating and humiliating if we cannot give the answer!

That is a wrong attitude, however human and natural. Who said that we must have all the answers? We are witnesses, not debaters. Moreover, the case does not depend on our ability to solve all problems, but on the witness of the Spirit along with us and through us.

But whether or not we have all the answers, we have *the answer,* and in private conversation it is our privilege to show how the Lord Jesus is the answer to every man's need. Behind many of the questions asked there is a longing to be assured of that very fact. The gentleman in the pulpit may say so in general terms, but in individual encounter we can make it definitive, and point the way. The questions of a scoffer may be out of our field of knowledge, but the questions of a seeker have an answer right at hand —in the Book. I have frequently discovered that the actual questions asked were really not so important as the questioner made out, nor even so important as he thought them to be. They were hurdles because he could not see beyond them; but when the Lord Jesus was presented, the insurmountable obstacle seemed to fall away and was forgotten. But he had had opportunity to ask his question, and the Saviour was set forth in connection with his own difficulty, and he was satisfied. When the Holy Spirit is at work, problems have a way of dissolving.

E. IT GETS AWAY FROM THE PROFESSIONAL IDEA.

When a housewife sees a salesman coming, her sales resistance surges up within her. If she opens the door, it is with a determination not to be "taken in" by sales talk. This man professionally represents his goods, which means that what he says must be discounted at least fifty per cent! Rightly or wrongly, that is the attitude of many to the professional salesman. Now if a neighbor came to the same housewife, showing the same article, paying it glowing tributes as the finest thing she had ever discovered in its field, the reaction would probably be entirely different. A satisfied customer is the best salesman. That, of course, is why commercial firms frantically seek personal testimonies for their products.

While evangelism is more than salesmanship, yet this same principle holds. A minister is not always in the best situation to witness. Many regard him as a "professional," and therefore to be taken at a discount. But a "satisfied customer," or neighbor, a friend, who has found the reality and the preciousness of Christ, and whose life demonstrates the fact, is in a place of advantage for personal witness. Admittedly a true minister by his sincerity and manifest earnestness will win through, but the fact remains that he has that extra obstacle to overcome. It is certain that the minister who confines his witness to the pulpit will not win — he *is* a professional. But the minister who joins the ranks of satisfied customers and engages in personal evangelism will be known as a man who cares, and to him men will listen.

Nominal, stagnant Christians naturally affirm that soul-winning is the minister's business. So said a young man to me when I was urging him to seek to lead others to Christ. He went so far as to declare that he would resent anyone other than a minister approaching him on such subjects. It was quite evident that he was putting up a defense for his own neglect of the sacred duty and blessed privilege committed to all Christians.

F. PERSONAL TOUCH SUCCEEDS WHERE OTHER METHODS FAIL.

The Shunammite woman who built a prophet's chamber for Elisha came to him one day with the heavy news that her young son was dead. The prophet sent his servant Gehazi posthaste to lay the staff upon the dead child's face, but there was no response. That was exactly as the mother expected, for she refused to return home with the servant, but insisted on Elisha himself accompanying her. On their arrival the prophet shut himself in the chamber with the child, and after praying, stretched himself upon the dead body. This he did twice, and the child gave a definite sign of life—he sneezed seven times![12] What the touch of the rod could not do, the personal contact accomplished, by the power of God. The rod is very good in its place, for stretching over waters and smiting rocks, but it does not take the place of the human touch.

One day John the Baptist, in the midst of his labors, caught sight of Jesus, and cried: "Behold the Lamb of God, which taketh away the sin of the world." The context suggests that these words were spoken to the multitude. The next day John was talking with two of his followers when again he saw Jesus. Pointing Him out he said to the two, "Behold the Lamb of God." Now the more elaborate

---

[12]II Kings 4:18-37.

and more public statement of the first day did not seem to send people scurrying after Jesus, but that simple, personal word to his two disciples struck a new chord in their hearts, and "they followed Jesus."[13]

As one who has preached for many years, I should hesitate to agree that preaching is not an effective instrument of soul-winning, especially when the Bible says that it is.[14] I admit that the statement with which we opened this chapter hurts a bit. But I freely acknowledge that I have preached my heart out to certain people with no apparent response, only to find them open and ready when I put myself out to see them personally.

There was a fellow-Scot whose name was John. He began coming to my church, I suppose, because we were from the same part of Scotland. He sorely needed the Lord, and I preached to him as if there were no one else in the congregation. One day I went to see him, not knowing how I would be received. He was asleep, because he was on the night shift. I left a note for him, written on a tract entitled, *Old John Is Dead, I Am New John.* A day or two later I received a piece of mail. Opening the envelope, I saw my tract returned. My heart sank. But I looked again and saw a piece of paper on which was written:

> O Jesus, I have promised
>   To serve Thee to the end.
> Be Thou forever near me,
>   My Master and my Friend.
> I shall not fear the battle,
>   If Thou art by my side,
> Nor wander from the pathway,
>   If Thou wilt be my Guide.

---

[13]John 1:29-37
[14]I Cor. 1:21.

> Oh, give me grace to follow
> My Saviour and my Friend.
>> An auld friend,
>> New John.

It was not the preaching, but the personal touch that won him.

QUESTIONS AND EXERCISES

1. Who made the statement that "the intensity of the appeal is in inverse proportion to the area covered"?
2. Discuss the statement that all can engage in personal evangelism.
3. Of whom was it said that "every social relation was a tie by which men might be drawn to Christ"?
4. What two contrary cravings are present in us all, which must be taken into account in evangelism?
5. List the advantages of personal evangelism given in this lesson, and add any other which you can suggest.

LESSON 7

The Sanctions of Personal Evangelism

A SANCTION is a consideration which enforces or urges obedience to some rule of action. A penalty attached to the breach of a law is a sanction. A reward offered for the fulfillment of a duty is a sanction. A name of authority attached to a call is a sanction. The word has also the connotation of permission, but that is a secondary meaning.

What considerations are there, then, to enforce the duty of personal witnessing for Christ?

A. *Indebtedness.*

"I am debtor," said the apostle Paul, "both to the Greeks, and to the Barbarians; both to the wise, and to the unwise."[1] Now there can be no doubt that Paul, as Saul of Tarsus, had derived some intellectual and cultural benefits from the Greek world, so that he was in some sense a debtor to the Greeks. But what did he ever gain from the Barbarians that he should owe them anything?

Debtorship comes in other ways than by benefits received from the party involved. In the medical profession, a man who discovers something which would contribute to the cure of a disease is required by the ethics of his profession to make it known. He is regarded as a debtor to all mankind with respect to that discovery. This obligation is based on the unity and solidarity of the human race.

---

[1] Rom. 1:14.

"None of us liveth to himself,"[2] saith the Scriptures, and the world of medicine, to this extent at least, recognizes this principle. There before me is a world of need; here in my hand is the cure, or at least an alleviation. By that I become a debtor.

Exactly that was the nature of Paul's debtorship, and we are one with him. Around us is a world of sinners, lost and undone. We have the answer: the Gospel of our Lord Jesus Christ. In such a case we are debtors to everyone who knows not Christ.

The four lepers hugging the walls of besieged Samaria decided to appeal to the pity of the Syrian army as the only possible hope of survival. When they arrived at the camp of the invading hosts, there were no Syrians to be seen. The sound of approaching armies had sent them scurrying for their lives. The amazed lepers started in on the booty, satisfying their hunger from the abandoned stores. Then they came to themselves and remembered that the discovery of this abundance made them debtors to the starving inhabitants of the city. So they hastened back to convey the good news to the keeper of the gates.[3]

We who have "tasted that the Lord is gracious"[4] have a debt to pay. We owe the good news to our friends and neighbors.

B. *Command.*

The last recorded command of the risen Saviour to His band of followers on the eve of His ascension to glory was: "Go ye into all the world, and preach the gospel to every creature."[5] There can be no doubt that that was a representative and inclusive command, indicating His will for

---

[2] Rom. 14:7.
[3] II Kings 7.
[4] I Peter 2:3.
[5] Mark 16:15.

all who would take His name upon them. It is evident
that no one person, or all of the little group to whom the
Lord spoke these words, could reach "every creature."
Every believer, then, shares the responsibility of carrying
out the Lord's command so long as there is one creature who
has not heard.

There are many ways in which we may share the task.
We may give of our means, we may pray, we may encourage those who go to the regions beyond, we may serve
in Christian institutions and help to train ministers and
missionaries, but all that does not release us from our personal share in the witnessing. No one man can go into all
the world, but each one can go into a part of it, if only to
the neighbor next door or round the corner.

That the command to witness does not necessarily imply
leaving home for the regions beyond is made clear in one
of our cherished Gospel incidents. The demoniac of Ga-
dara, out of whom Jesus cast a host of evil spirits, earnestly
desired to accompany the Lord in His itinerant ministry.
Perhaps he wished to get away from that part of the country associated with his former terrible bondage; perhaps
he felt the shame of his former life so that he shrank from
living among the people who knew him; or perhaps he
just felt the need of Christ's presence as security against a
possible return of his evil state. Whatever the motive, his
request was denied. Instead, he was given a commission:
"Go home to thy friends, and tell them how great things
the Lord hath done for thee, and hath had compassion on
thee."[6] No doubt it would have been easier for him to go
into the work "professionally," but the command meant
for him to stay home and do personal work. Home territory
is the best proving-ground for the Christian.

---

[6]Mark 5:17-19.

C. *Appointment.*

British merchants and manufacturers regard it as a great honor to be able to emboss their letterheads with the words, *By Appointment.* This means, of course, that their product has been accepted for royal use, so that henceforth they are manufacturing goods for the king, or for the queen, as the case may be. Just recently, I noticed on a jar of marmalade from Scotland the words, "By appointment, manufacturers of preserves to His late Majesty King George VI." Even the memory of past honors is cherished.

We are more signally honored than those privileged merchants. One more royal than the most regal of earth has appointed us to serve Him. His own words, addressed primarily to the apostolic band, but including every believer, are: "Ye have not chosen me, but I have chosen you, and ordained you, that ye should go and bring forth fruit, and that your fruit should remain."[7] Now while I believe that the fruit of godly character is here in view,[8] I am equally sure that the fruit of "reproduction" through faithful and effective witnessing is not out of sight.

Such divine ordination ought to give us courage and a holy boldness. I have never heard of a British merchant being ashamed of the royal appointment, or refusing it. They will emblazon the royal coat-of-arms over their place of business, and accept the appointment as a signal to forge ahead and produce the best in their field. So our appointment by Christ should be an incentive to us to fulfill the commission in such fashion that He will say, "Well done."

D. *Example.*

Personal evangelism is not a twentieth-century invention. It is quite after the New Testament order. There we do not

---
[7]John 15:16.
[8]*See* Gal. 5:22, 23.

find the work of witnessing confined to the apostles, or the "clergy" if you will. It was a task in which all were expected to engage.

The Book of Acts tells us of a veritable hurricane of persecution which struck the church. Apparently Saul of Tarsus, the youthful and fiery Pharisee, was a prime mover, or at least a chief agent, in the persecution. So fierce did it become in Jerusalem, that "they were all scattered abroad throughout the regions of Judea and Samaria, except the apostles."[9] Notice that phrase, *except the apostles.* The ministers "stuck it out," but the rank and file of the believers fled the city. Now we look at verse 4 of the same chapter: "Therefore they that were scattered abroad went everywhere preaching the word." We must not be misled by that word *preaching.* It does not necessarily mean preaching sermons—not even standing before a group of people. It equally applies to telling a single individual, and there can be no doubt that there was far more of that done by these persecuted, scattered Christians than formal preaching.

It is interesting to follow the developments from that informal witnessing. We turn to Acts 11:19, and we see these same dispersed Christians traveling as far as "Phenice, and Cyprus, and Antioch." Those who reached Antioch (Syrian Antioch) could not restrain themselves from witnessing to the Greeks there, with the result that they suddenly found themselves with a Gentile church on their hands! Now Peter, under strong pressure from the Lord, had given the Word to the Roman Cornelius,[10] but the witness had not really burst its Jewish banks to overflow the Gentile world. The instruments of the larger movement were these persecuted refugees. Peter had slain his

---

[9]Acts 8:1.   [10]Acts 10.

thousands, but these their ten thousands.

Surely these things are our examples. Why does the Lord have His people scattered throughout the world instead of locked up in some Utopian community? Just because He wants witnesses everywhere. Every Christian is a "cell" for the propagation of the Gospel in the midst of a non-Christian society. The work will not be done by "professionals," apostles, or ministers, but by believing men and women—"you in your small corner, and I in mine."

E. *Love.*

This is the mightiest of all sanctions. "The love of Christ constraineth us,"[11] said the apostle Paul, and I like to put alongside that David Livingstone's explanation of his willingness to endure Africa's dangers and discomforts and diseases and hardships and discouragements when he might have remained at home and enjoyed the honors that men were ready to heap on him. Echoing the words of the apostle, he replied, "The love of Christ compelled me." These words are inscribed below the rough-hewn cross made from a block of the tree beneath which Livingstone's heart was buried in Africa, and set up in the shrine of the National Livingstone Memorial in Blantyre, Scotland. It is one of the most eloquent items of the entire memorial.

Love is a compelling force. We may acknowledge our indebtedness, recognize the command, accept the appointment, and admit the example set for us, and still keep silent. But if love takes over, there will be an inner drive which we shall find irresistible—we shall not want to resist. Or it is possible to act from the sense of indebtedness, in obedience to the command, under the terms of the appointment, and in keeping with the example, and still do all without love. In such case our witnessing will be formal,

---

[11] II Cor. 5:14.

forced, frigid, and the results are likely to be less than meager. We may be gifted in approach, apt in presentation, enthusiastic in nature, but the lack of love will cancel out our talents and leave us ineffective. "If I speak with the tongues of men and of angels, but have not love, I am become sounding brass, or a clanging cymbal."[12]

Love is the real basis of all true service. We remember that in Peter's recall to the apostolate after his tragic denial of the Lord, the triple recommissioning was based on a triple confession of love.[13] "Lovest thou me? . . . Feed my sheep." That is the order, and the same holds for going out after the lost sheep.

Admittedly we do not have this love by nature. We may have natural compassion and natural kindliness and natural courage and natural enthusiasm, but what natural love we have is not the love that counts in this greatest of all service. But it is available. "The love of God is shed abroad in our hearts by the Holy Ghost which is given unto us."[14]

Questions and Exercises

1. What is meant by a *sanction?*
2. List and explain the five sanctions of personal evangelism.
3. Discuss different senses in which we may be debtors, and apply to the work of evangelism.
4. Evaluate the statement: Home territory is the best proving-ground for the Christian.
5. Where in the New Testament do we have a notable example of extensive witnessing on the part of the rank and file of the church?
6. Which is the mightiest sanction of all, and how may we know its constraining power?

---

[12] I Cor. 13:1 (A.S.V.).
[13] John 21:15-17.
[14] Rom. 5:5.

LESSON 8

Qualifications of the Soul-Winner

IN THE LESSON on "Advantages of Personal Evangelism" we said that anyone can do it. That statement now calls for some modification. While all can do it in the sense of its being within reach of all, there are certain qualifications which one must have before he is equipped to do this work as it ought to be done. We shall have to admit that many Christians do not possess these qualifications, but, on the other hand, these qualifications are attainable by all, through the grace of God, and in measure as they are attained, one's effectiveness will increase.

C. H. Spurgeon was not only a great preacher, but a great soul-winner. He has offered us his suggestions[1] on the qualifications for this sacred task, dividing them into two categories—Godward and Manward:

1. *Godward*
   Holiness of character
   Spiritual life
   Humility
   Living faith
   Earnestness
   Simplicity of heart
   Complete surrender

2. *Manward*
   Knowledge
   Sincerity
   Evident earnestness
   Love
   Unselfishness
   Seriousness
   Tenderness

[1]C. H. Spurgeon, *The Soul-Winner* (Westwood, N. J.: Revell), pp. 39, 65.

It would be very profitable to contemplate all these qualities, and we may well covet them all. I think, however, that they can all be included in five main propositions.

A. *The Soul-Winner Must Be a Man of Character.*

The apostle Paul was most insistent upon the personal character of the servant of God, and in his letters to Timothy he reverts to that subject again and again. To Timothy himself he says with great emphasis and earnestness, "Take heed unto thyself."[2] The spiritual condition is so much a determining factor in the response of the hearer that it becomes a matter of primary importance. It is the man who is careful to have no stain upon his character that is "a vessel unto honor, sanctified, and meet for the master's use."[3]

God, being a holy God, uses clean vessels for sacred purposes. The ablutions of the priests of old, required of them before handling the vessels of the sanctuary, are a parable of the moral purity which God demands of those who would handle His holy Gospel. There are indeed some tasks in which God uses strange instruments. He used a dumb ass to reprove a willful prophet.[4] He used wicked kings to scourge his disobedient people again and again. He uses the Devil, turning the designs of the adversary into means of accomplishing His own good will. But He does not entrust the holy things into the hands of beasts, devils, or sinners. These He commits to clean hands, and if we handle them with defiled fingers, let us not be surprised if the Lord's severe chastenings come upon us.

I once heard an evangelist in a sermon on soul-winning

---

[2] I Tim. 4:16.
[3] II Tim. 2:21.
[4] Num. 22:21-34.

ask the question: "Should a Christian try to win souls if his life is not right?" His conclusion was: "I think God will forgive you for trying to win souls even if you are not what you should be." I can only hope that this was said in the heat of the moment, and did not truly represent the evangelist's thinking. What ought to have been said was: The Christian's first duty is to get right with God and men, and then, out of a shining life, go forth as a clean vessel, "prepared unto every good work."[5]

We must remember that the Gospel is more than an offer of forgiveness and a promise of Heaven. "Thou shalt call his name Jesus: for he shall save his people *from their sins.*"[6] A man who is living in sin cannot proclaim that Gospel. How can we offer to others what has not become a reality to ourselves? It is hypocrisy, and nothing so repels men as the "testimony" of a hypocrite. Of course one may do his witnessing where he is not known, but it will lack the ring of conviction, and it will lack the power of the Holy Spirit; and even if a suave manner seems to give him a measure of success for a while, the truth will out, and the work of the Gospel will suffer.

On the other hand, a Christlike character is an argument against which there is no answer. It is the most convincing testimony that can be given. In Sault Ste Marie, Canada, there was an immigration officer[7] whose life shone with the reality of Christ. One day he telephoned me to say he was bringing two men to see me. On their arrival I learned that they had just received the Lord Jesus. When I asked them what had persuaded them to take this step,

---

[5]II Tim. 2:21.
[6]Matt. 1:21 (emphasis ours).
[7]I am sure it would not be out of place to give this man's name. He was David Lynn, now with the Lord. His quiet, radiant testimony at the border brought many to Christ.

one of them promptly replied: "I have been watching this man [pointing to my friend] for months, and his life convinced me that I needed what he had." That is what counts.

The character which qualifies one for soul-winning is something more than standard moral conduct, something more than an avoidance of stealing, lying, fornication, and such like. Basically it is likeness to Christ, showing itself in patience, kindness, meekness—indeed, in all that the apostle Paul calls "the fruit of the Spirit."[8]

This does not mean that we must wait for sinless perfection before we begin personal evangelism. If we wait for that, we shall wait until there is no more evangelism for us to engage in. But it does mean that we shall be allowing no known sin in our lives, that we shall be submitting to the disciplines of the Holy Spirit in order to have our ways conformed to the will of God, and that we shall be waiting in our Lord's presence until we go forth with something of His beauty upon us.

> Let the beauty of Jesus be seen in me,
> All His wonderful passion and purity.
> O Thou Spirit Divine, fill this temple of Thine,[9]
> Till the beauty of Jesus be seen in me.
>
> — ALBERT OSBORN

B. *The Soul-Winner Must Be a Man of Complete Passion.* We have heard of the passion for souls, and we generally associate the phrase with the earnest desire to see sinners converted. Actually, that is only one-half of the passion for souls. The other half is an equal concern to see the saints, the converted, perfected in Christ. What would you think of a young couple who were very eager to have children, but gave no thought to the development of the chil-

---

[8]Gal. 5:22, 23.
[9]Third line changed by Homer Hammontree.

dren after they arrived? So it is not enough to strive for the salvation of the lost. We must also seek the sanctification and growth of the saved. The two together make a complete passion for souls. The first without the second is likely to produce shallow work. The second without the first can dry up the springs of evangelism.

Paul had a complete passion for souls. He yearned over the unsaved, and equally over the saints. Listen to his heart cry for those who knew not the Lord Jesus: "I say the truth in Christ, I lie not, my conscience also bearing me witness in the Holy Ghost, That I have great heaviness and continual sorrow in my heart. For I could wish that myself were accursed from Christ for my brethren, my kinsmen according to the flesh."[10] But his yearning over the saints is just as intense. He actually suffers on the behalf of the Galatian Christians, to whom he writes: "My little children, of whom I travail in birth again until Christ be formed in you."[11] Let us covet to have a full passion for souls.

Now we should analyze the passion for souls and see just what its elements are. In other words, what constitutes the passion for souls?

1. The first and basic element is love for Christ. We have already mentioned the place of love in our lesson on the "Sanctions of Personal Evangelism." Here it ought to be stressed again. Notice now that it is love for Christ, not love for souls, which comes first. When the Lord Jesus was recommissioning Peter after his sad failure, He did not say to him, "Peter, do you love my sheep?—Then go and feed them." Rather He said, "Lovest thou me? . . . Feed my sheep."[12]

---

[10]Rom. 9:1-3.
[11]Gal. 4:19.
[12]John 21:15-17.

David Brainerd was an ardent soul-winner, but he knew its primary element. In his diary, he writes: "I poured out my soul for the world. My soul was constrained not so much for souls as such, but rather for Christ's kingdom that it might appear in the world, that God might be known to be God in the whole earth."[13] See, then, how his prayer for souls rises out of his love for Christ.

Another example was the great German theologian, Tholuck. Here is his own testimony. "I adopted for my own life the famous motto of Count Zinzendorf (I have but one passion and that is He, and He alone). To bring back souls to Christ was from that time the daily, nay, the hourly problem, as well as the joy of my life."[14]

There is reason for this. If our passion for souls is based on nothing more than love for the sinner or love for the saint, we are going to lose our passion, for we shall find saints and sinners alike very unlovely at times, and we shall be thoroughly discouraged, but if everything revolves around Christ we shall be kept from disillusionment. He always is lovely, and as we look at Him, and our hearts go out in love to Him, any task done for Him will be done with zest and eagerness.

2. The second element in the passion for souls, and always rising out of the first, is concern for souls. You see then what many take for a complete passion for souls is only one element in it, and that the second, not the first.

It was because the love of Christ constrained him that Paul was so concerned for his kinsfolk.[15] His willingness to take the curse if only it might be for their salvation arose out of his drinking deeply of the love of Christ.

---

[13]Jonathan Edwards, *The Life and Diary of David Brainerd* (Chicago 10: Moody Press), p. 129.
[14]Report of Evangelical Alliance Conference held in New York, October 2-12, 1873.
[15]Rom. 9:3.

Paul's concern was not confined to the Jews, but extended to the Gentiles. We have this remarkable portrait of Paul in Athens: "Now while Paul waited for them at Athens, his spirit was stirred in him, when he saw the city wholly given to idolatry."[16] That word *stirred* is a strong one in the Greek. From it we have our English word *paroxysm*, and it would not be an exaggeration to use that word here. Paul was thrown into a paroxysm in the spirit. What so affected him? First, he saw in all this idolatry God dishonored, and then he saw man degraded. He was ashamed and grieved at the sight and longed for the salvation of those who, created in the image of God, had so marred that image.

In his remarkable poem, *Saint Paul*, Meyer describes this passion of the apostle Paul.

Oft when the Word is on me to deliver,
　Lifts the illusion, and the truth lies bare;
Desert or throng, the city or the river
　Melts in a lucid paradise of air.

Only like souls I see the men thereunder,
　Bound who should conquer, slaves who should be kings,
Hearing their one hope with an empty wonder,
　Sadly contented with a show of things.

Then with a rush, th' intolerable craving
　Shivers throughout me, like a trumpet call,
Oh, to save these, to perish for their saving,
　Die for their life, be offered for them all!

Moses was also a man of like passion with Saint Paul. When the judgment of God hung over the sinning nation like the Sword of Damocles, Moses stepped into the breach to plead with God on their behalf. Listen to the intensity of his pleading: "Oh, this people have sinned a great sin, and

---

[16]Acts 17:16.

have made them gods of gold. Yet now, if thou wilt forgive their sin—; and if not, blot me, I pray thee, out of thy book which thou hast written."[17] Moses actually offers himself to bear the judgment of Israel if only that would secure their forgiveness and salvation. Surely here we see a concern for souls enough to make us ashamed.

3. The third element in this passion is a sense of urgency. We blame the sinner for his procrastination in accepting Christ, but how often do we have to plead guilty of procrastination in witnessing to them! We need to apply to ourselves some of the verses that we quote to sinners, as for instance, "Behold, now is the accepted time; behold, now is the day of salvation."[18] This everlasting "now" has gripped the soul of the true soul-winner.

When I was a boy, I attended a series of meetings where an ex-sailor, Sidney Watson, was preaching. The remembrance is especially vivid because at that time he was on crutches as a result of a back injury sustained when he caught a woman leaping from a burning building. His conversion, as he himself told it, took place when he was serving on H.M.S. "Zealous." At one of the English ports another sailor, John Martin, joined the ship as a sailmaker. Martin was not ten minutes on board till he was witnessing to Watson. His sense of urgency was revealed in his own words, which Watson never forgot: "I have got to see the first leftenant,[19] get my orders from the bosun,[20] change my clothes, pick up my mess, and take over my stores, but your soul's salvation, Sidney Watson, is of more consequence than everything else." Here was the sense of urgency which always accompanies a passion for souls.

---

[17]Exod. 32:31, 32.
[18]II Cor. 6:2.
[19]First Lieutenant.
[20]Boatswain.

4. The fourth element is a sense of responsibility. No one with a passion for souls will ever ask Cain's question, "Am I my brother's keeper?"[21] We know that we are.

When the Jews of the restoration fell into the sin of mixed marriages and other evils which threatened their national existence, Ezra gave himself to prayer, with confession and weeping before God. Then one of the princes of the people came to Ezra, saying, "Arise; for this matter belongeth unto thee."[22] That is an excellent motto for the soul-winner. It was exactly this that made D. L. Moody the soul-winner that he was. He knew that it was his business. He was conscious that a responsibility rested upon him.

5. The fifth element is a sense of call. We are not just taking this on ourselves as a matter of charity or pity. We have received a commission. What the risen Lord said to the disciples in the upper room applies equally to us: "As my Father hath sent me, even so I send you."[23] We share also the charge specially given to Peter that day when he lent his boat to Jesus and for wages received a great draught of fishes. When, in his astonishment, and with a profound sense of his unworthiness, he cried out: "Depart from me; for I am a sinful man, O Lord," Jesus answered him: "Fear not; from henceforth thou shalt catch men."[24]

This sense of call not only gives meaning to life, but it also upholds us in times when we would be tempted to give it all up. Remember that the passion for souls is not all emotion. Emotion fluctuates, and there are times when we need the steadying influence of this realization that we are called and sent.

---

[21]Gen. 4:9.
[22]Ezra 10:4.
[23]John 20:21.
[24] Luke 5:8-10.

C. *The Soul-Winner Must Be a Man of Conviction.*

Unless we are convinced beyond all peradventure of doubt, we shall be ineffective in our witnessing. That does not mean that we shall necessarily be exempt from temptations to doubt. The adversary will use every occasion to plant thoughts of uncertainty in our minds, but if we have the answer of the Word, and the witness of the Spirit within, we shall not entertain the suggestions of unbelief but quickly dismiss them. Conviction of the truth, then, is a necessary qualification for this task. Any wavering on our part will not produce a glowing witness, nor strike fire in the hearts of others. Three convictions are required of every soul-winner:

1. There must be no question about the condition of the sinner. If we are not sure that men are lost, we shall have no great urge to seek their salvation. To say the least, our sense of urgency will be greatly diminished if we entertain a secret belief that after all God will find some other way of saving men who depart this life without faith in Christ.

2. We must harbor no doubt as to the truth of the Gospel, and the sufficiency of Christ to save any man. Paul wrote with glowing confidence: "I am not ashamed of the gospel of Christ: for it is the power of God unto salvation to everyone that believeth."[25] The apostle could not conceive of any believing in vain, or of Christ failing to save to the uttermost all that should come to Him.

No salesman can be very successful who is not himself "sold" on his goods. I remember a good friend of mine who, for very legitimate reasons, changed from one firm to another several times. But whatever firm he represented, he was absolutely convinced that no product in the same field was the equal of what he was selling. Such assurance

---

[25]Rom. 1:16.

Isaiah 55:10-11
Numbers 23:19
Luke 19:10

concerning the Gospel is a basic requirement for the soul-winner. We must be convinced that there is no case beyond the piactice of the Great Physician, that no sinner is beyond the reach of our Saviour's grace. Unless we can meet the most abandoned sinner with a ringing certainty that Christ is fully equal to the need, we are defeated before we begin.

3. We must entertain no fear regarding God's acceptance of all who come. Let us believe in election with all the ardor of our souls. But if our belief in election hinders us from inviting sinners to Christ, or makes us uncertain of their reception when they come, our view of election is off balance. Our Lord Jesus did not hesitate to extend an all-covering invitation: "Come unto me, all ye that labor and are heavy laden,"[26] and He did not modify His promise, "I will give you rest," with an uncertain, "if you happen to be of the elect." Rather He issued a glad assurance, "Him that cometh to me I will in no wise cast out."[27] No seeker will ever come to the Saviour and be disappointed or turned away. Of that we must be certain.

D. *The Soul-Winner Must Be a Man of Understanding.*

1. He must have an understanding of his message. One who is vague in his conception of the Gospel will consequently be vague in his presentation of it, and he is liable to send people away with a complete misconception. This is why we devoted an entire lesson (Lesson 2) to "The Message of Evangelism," which ought to be thoroughly mastered. Pray that the Holy Spirit will enlighten your understanding so that you may be crystal clear on the truth of the Gospel.

2. He must have an understanding of men. Our Lord

[26]Matt. 11:28.
[27]John 6:37.

uses a vivid word for soul-winning, and one which suggests
the need for great understanding. He said to Peter: "Fear
not; from henceforth thou shalt catch men."[28] That word
catch means "take alive." It is used only one other place
in the New Testament, where we are told that the Devil
is in the business of taking men alive.[29] There can be no
doubt that he has understanding of men, and knows how
to deceive them. We too must acquire an understanding
of men if we are to be God's instruments in undeceiving
them.

A good fisherman studies the habits of fish, to know which
bait to use, whether to use a float or a sinker, whether it is
necessary to cast lightly, and many other items. When I
was a boy, I used to go with my pals to the river to catch
flounders. A long line, a hook, a worm, and a weight were
all we needed. We threw the line, let it sink, and waited.
Catching hill trout in the rushing streams of the Ochils was
a very different matter.

As fish are different, and need different treatment, so are
men. Men do not all respond to the same approach or the
same appeal. This is apparent in the conversions of the
New Testament. With Saul of Tarsus the appeal was
particularly to the will, as is seen in his immediate response,
"What wilt thou have me to do?"[30] The approach to the
Ethiopian eunuch was through the mind, "Understandest
thou what thou readest?"[31] Lydia was won in the emotional
sphere, "Whose heart the Lord opened."[32]

Evangeline Booth had amazing understanding of people,
and as a result won multitudes whom other less wise Chris-

------

[28]Luke 5:10.
[29]II Tim. 2:26 (A.S.V., marg.).
[30]Acts 9:6.
[31]Acts 8:30.
[32]Acts 16:14.

tians could never have reached. On one occasion at a street
meeting a rough man threw a rock which made a gash in
her arm. Without hesitation she went up to him and
handed him a piece of cloth (perhaps a handkerchief),
saying, "Here. Bandage this. You did it. You fix it." The
"tough guy" wilted, became a fast friend, and yielded to
the Lord, later becoming a member of the "Army."[33] By
such understanding methods she broke down prejudices.
She was careful not to offend the spark of self-respect left
in the most depraved men and women.

3. He must have an understanding of situations. We all
know the old adage, "Fools rush in where angels fear to
tread." But we go on rushing in! There are times when the
most effective speech is silence, when a warm handclasp
will speak more eloquently than words.

On the other hand, we must guard against being so
tactful that we never make contact or come to grips. There
is danger of excusing ourselves on the ground that the
time was inopportune, when in our hearts we know very
well that we just fell down on the job.

The wisdom which is from above, which God has promised to give to those who ask,[34] will make one alert to situations, whether it be time to speak or time to be silent, time
to stay or time to go, time to press for decision or time to
drop a seed with a prayer and a tear.

E. *The Soul-Winner Must Be a Man of Unction.*

Soul-winning is a divine work. In it God graciously uses
men — redeemed men. But always "we have this treasure
in earthen vessels, that the excellency of the power may be
of God, and not of us."[35] Now God fits for this divine work
by bestowing His Holy Spirit upon us, not that the Holy

---

[33]*The Reader's Digest,* August, 1947.
[34]James 3:17; 1:5.
[35]II Cor. 4:7.

Spirit may be our servant to supply us what we want on demand, but that the Holy Spirit may master and control us,
and so make us the channels of the power of God. This is
what we mean by unction, or anointing. We read that "God
anointed Jesus of Nazareth with the Holy Ghost and with
power: who went about doing good . . . for God was with
him."[36] But what does the Lord Jesus say about His own
ministry? That He did, not His own will, but the will of Him
that sent Him,[37] and that the works were not His, but the
Father's who had sent Him.[38] For the Lord Jesus this was
condescension, for as the eternal Son of God He has no
need, no deficiency, yet He stooped to be an obedient, de-
pendent servant. We, on the other hand, are exceedingly
deficient, but the Holy Spirit is God's answer to our deficiency, as we walk and work in His control.

1. We need the Holy Spirit for leading. Our Lord was
so led. "And Jesus being full of the Holy Ghost returned
from Jordan, and was led by the Spirit into the wilderness."[39] If we are led by the Holy Spirit—which is a mark
of the sons of God[40]—we shall not be engaging in fruitless
endeavors, leading to disappointment and discouragement
and disaster, but the Holy Spirit will be bringing prepared
hearts and a prepared messenger together, with blessed
results. Every prayerful pastor has had the experience
again and again, in going to a home, to find a need of
which he was ignorant, and after ministering to that need,
having the party concerned say, "God certainly sent you
here today." So it may be in soul-winning, if we know the
unction of the Holy Spirit.

---

[36]Acts 10:38.
[37]John 5:30.
[38]John 14:10.
[39]Luke 4:1.
[40]Rom. 8:14.

2. We need the Holy Spirit for utterance. When the apostles, Peter and John, returned from a round with the Sanhedrin and reported to the church the threatenings of the council, the assembled group gave themselves to prayer, particularly asking for boldness in the face of the rising opposition. Now notice how their prayer was answered: "And they were all filled with the Holy Ghost, and they spake the word of God with boldness."[41] The Holy Spirit gave the utterance, when human frailty would have been tempted to silence.

When it is time to speak, the Holy Ghost will give us also the needed boldness and the word to speak, if He has control. How tongue-tied we can be when it comes to speaking about the Lord Jesus! A steady flow of conversation on other themes becomes an embarrassed silence, or a limping stammering affair. Our thoughts suddenly become confused, we feel nervous, and utter a few incoherent words, and wish we were a thousand miles away! But with the unction of the Holy Spirit there comes a wonderful calm and poise, apt Scriptures are brought to mind, and we find ourselves witnessing with glowing heart.

We can, of course, engage in a religious argument without the unction of the Spirit. Maybe we can even win the argument—and lose the soul. On the other hand, men who could not win an argument have often won a soul by refusing to argue, and quietly witnessing. It is related that C. T. Studd was once traveling to China on a ship whose captain was an ardent infidel, and who had studied the Bible with the sole intention of confusing simple Christians, especially the missionaries who frequently sailed on his vessel. On learning that another missionary was on board, the unbelieving captain sought out Mr. Studd and

---

"Acts 4:31.

started on his usual line of ridicule. Studd, instead of arguing, put his arm around the captain and said, "But, my friend, I have a peace that passeth all understanding, and a joy that nothing can take away." The hardened sailor replied, "You're a lucky dog," and walked away. A few days later he became a rejoicing believer in the Lord Jesus Christ.[42]

3. We need the Holy Spirit for power. "Not by might, nor by power, but by my spirit, saith the Lord of hosts."[43] Such was the word of the Lord to Zerubbabel in the days of the rebuilding of the temple, and the same principle holds in the days of the building of the living temple. In commissioning His disciples, and through them all who should follow after, our Lord declared: "Ye shall receive power, after that the Holy Ghost is come upon you: and ye shall be witnesses unto me."[44] Power is not granted to us apart from the Holy Spirit. It never becomes our possession. It is always the attribute of the Holy Spirit, and flows through us as channels.

> Channels only, blessed Master!
> But with all Thy wondrous power
> Flowing through us, Thou canst use us
> Every day, and every hour.
>
> —MARY E. MAXWELL

"He that believeth on me . . . out of his belly shall flow rivers of living water. But this spake he of the Spirit."[45]

---

[42]This incident was related in detail by Mr. Studd in a letter to his mother, and is found on pages 52-53 of the biography by his son-in-law, Norman P. Grubb, C. T. Studd, Cricketer and Pioneer (London: Religious Tract Society).
[43]Zech. 4:6.
[44]Acts 1:8.
[45]John 7:38, 39.

QUESTIONS AND EXERCISES

1. Into what two categories does C. H. Spurgeon divide the qualifications of the soul-winner, and what does he include in each?
2. "Should a Christian try to win souls if his life is not right?" Discuss and answer this question.
3. What is meant by a complete passion for souls? Show how Paul gave evidence of such a complete passion.
4. Of what three truths must we be absolutely certain if we are to be effective soul-winners?
5. In what three areas must we have understanding in order to do effective work?
6. What two New Testament passages speak of taking men alive? Explain and compare them.
7. What is meant by *unction*, and what is its value to the soul-winner?

Difficulties in Personal Evangelism

TWO FACTS should be settled in our minds immediately to keep us from false expectations ending in disillusionment and discouragement. One is, soul-winning is not easy; the other is, it will not become easy. Even those who seem to have a remarkable gift in this respect have their struggles; and practice, however it may improve our technique, never reduces soul-winning to an easy formula.

There are several factors involved which make the work of personal evangelism always difficult. Four of these factors we shall consider.

A. *Ourselves.*

Every man is his own greatest problem, and we certainly stand in our own way when it comes to winning souls.

1. Our lukewarmness, for one thing, is a constant drag. The apostle Paul exhorts us to be "fervent in spirit,"[1] or as another has rendered it, "always at boiling point in the spirit." Not many of us can claim that we have attained to that happy estate. More of us, if we are honest, will feel that we come within the condemnation of the Laodiceans, and that, if the Lord were to deal with us as our condition calls for, He would spue us out of His mouth.[2] Our lack of fervor induces an apathy which is hard to conquer. How we need to call on the Holy Spirit for a baptism of fire!

[1] Rom. 12:11.
[2] Rev. 3:16.

2. Our variableness of disposition and temper militates against a steady work of soul-winning, making us spasmodic in our efforts. We can be ablaze with zeal today, and utterly cold tomorrow. We only have to examine our own ways to acknowledge the need of Paul's exhortation: "Therefore, my beloved brethren, be ye steadfast, unmovable, always abounding in the work of the Lord, forasmuch as ye know that your labor is not in vain in the Lord."[3] It is true that some are more temperamental than others, and in them the difficulty is aggravated, but we all need the steady control of the Holy Spirit to overcome this ebb-and-flow way of living.

3. Unpreparedness of mind and heart through the neglect of waiting upon God is a difficulty known by all too many of us. Even such a godly man as Robert Murray M'Cheyne complained of this difficulty. He has this to say in his diary: "Often when I sleep long, or meet with others early, and then have family prayer and breakfast and forenoon callers, it is eleven or twelve o'clock before I begin secret prayer. This is a wretched system. . . . Family prayer loses much of its power and sweetness; *and I can do no good to those who come to seek for me.*"[4] The other side of the picture is given by Bishop Hall: "If my heart be early seasoned with His presence, it will savor of Him all day after."[5] How, then, can we expect to be in readiness for the sacred task if we rarely commune in secret with God?

4. Perhaps fear is our most formidable difficulty. Where a thousand fire one's courage, a solitary individual will often make him quail. This fear may assume various forms

---

[3] I Cor. 15:58.
[4] Andrew A. Bonar, *Memoir and Remains of R. M. M'Cheyne* (Edinburgh: Oliphant, Anderson, and Ferrier), p. 156. (Emphasis ours—J.C.M.)
[5] Quoted by Horatius Bonar in *Words to the Winners of Souls* (New York: American Tract Society), p. 23.

—fear to offend, fear of saying the wrong thing, fear of
ridicule, fear of being worsted in discussion, fear of being
rebuffed. Most of the time it is just indefinable fear. We
rebuke ourselves, we tell ourselves that with the Lord on
our side we have nothing to fear, but we go on fearing, and
secretly despise ourselves for it. We surely need the perfect
love that casts out fear,[6] and the boldness of the Holy Spirit.[7]

5. We are very much creatures of extremes. We see
some zealous souls manifesting a complete lack of wisdom,
and to all appearance harming the very cause which they
have eagerly espoused, and their tactless boldness drives
us to the other extreme of overcaution. It is hard for us
to find the happy mean, the right balance.

B. *The Unconverted.*

Even Christians are difficult to deal with, especially when
it comes to touching their pet sins. It is no easy thing,
then, to deal with the unconverted on such a revolutionary
matter as conversion. If we remember some things which
are told us in the Bible concerning the natural man, we
shall not be surprised at the difficulty of our task, but
rather we shall make up our minds that what we seek to
accomplish is possible only by the power of God.

1. The human nature with which we are dealing is natively incapable of apprehending the things of God. Our
Lord said to Nicodemus, a learned, upright, religious man,
"Except a man be born again, he cannot see the kingdom of
God."[8] Notice that word *see.* The kingdom of God is something foreign to his vision and his apprehension. The apostle
Paul enlarges on this fact: "But the natural man receiveth
not the things of the Spirit of God: for they are foolishness unto him: neither can he know them, because

[6]I John 4:18.
[7]Acts 4:31.
[8]John 3:3.

they are spiritually discerned."[9] The unconverted man does not have that peculiar faculty which enables him to understand the things of God. That is why it is such folly to put any stock in a man's religious opinions because he happens to be a great scientist or a great philosopher or a great mind in any earthly sphere. Unless he is "born from above" his great mind is as dark as night with respect to eternal truth. It is only as the Holy Spirit accompanies the word at our lips that we can expect any understanding to dawn on the minds of sinners.

2. The human nature with which we are dealing is natively at enmity with God. We do not mean that it was so in the beginning. As God created man, there was a perfect affinity between the two, but the entrance of sin drove man from his Creator and made him the enemy of God. The atheist, the infidel, the blasphemer and other such profane persons outwardly show their enmity; but less voluble sinners, even if they dress themselves up in the respectable garments of morality and religion, are still alienated and enemies in their minds,[10] as their conduct reveals. They may pay formal respects to God so long as God stays at a respectable distance from them; but if God comes too near and touches their lives, they resent the interference. They may be glad enough to know that there is a God who will ultimately bring everything out all right, but they will not have a God who demands obedience, who claims the right to govern in the life of the individual.

Thus it is something more than "sales resistance" with which the soul-winner has to contend. It is a deep-seated antagonism, nurtured through long generations, which can be overturned only by the power of the Holy Spirit.

---

[9] I Cor. 2:14.
[10] Col. 1:21.

3. Men's minds are full of ideas which are utterly contrary to the truth of the Gospel, and to these ideas they will cling with their last breath apart from the mighty work of the Spirit of God in enlightening and loosing them. For instance, who is going to be willing to regard himself as a lost, depraved, helpless sinner when he has been accustomed to think in terms of the natural goodness of man? Or who will be persuaded that he is on his way to Hell when he has entertained shallow thoughts of the goodness of God, apart from all considerations of righteousness and justice? Or who will consent to say, "Nothing in my hand I bring, Simply to thy cross I cling," when he has fed his ego with the doctrine of the sufficiency of man?

But we have almost trespassed on our next point.

C. *Our Message.*

We shall have to repeat what has just been said, but now from the point of view of the message we have to deliver rather than from the angle of those to whom we deliver it. It seems strange, indeed, to say that the most wonderful, the most blessed news ever sent from Heaven to earth should constitute a difficulty for the soul-winner, but there are elements in our message which stir human resentment deeply.

1. The Gospel regards men as sinners, worthy of Hell. For sure, this is not the Gospel, but the Gospel was given for men in that condition, and because all men were in that condition. So, to receive the Gospel, men must come to believe and acknowledge, "vile and full of sin I am." A Gospel which predicates that, to use the language of the world, has two strikes against it from the start. To regard men in this light is unpalatable to their pride and their self-righteousness.

2. The Gospel treats men as helpless, incapable of contributing anything to their own salvation. This is another stunning blow. Men want help, and are frequently willing to accept help, but it must be a type of help which recognizes and supplements their own efforts. We know how many countries have sought the help of the United States since World War II, but they want it in such fashion as not to reflect on their own sovereignty and their own sufficiency. We are all more or less sensitive in such matters. But the Gospel recognizes no contribution from men. It requires that men confess that they are utterly bankrupt, and that they accept a total salvation to which they have contributed absolutely nothing.

3. The Gospel ignores all that men reckon as merit. Men put great store by their philanthropies, their service contributions to the community, their religious affiliations, and reason that these ought to have some weight with God in reckoning up the balance. Moreover, there are religious institutions, such as the Roman Church, which lay great stress on the merit system. Therefore when men come with their hands laden with their merits, only to discover that the Gospel makes no place whatever for their treasured offerings, it is a humiliating and confounding experience. The natural reaction is resentment and antagonism.

4. The Gospel rejects all human reformation. Human religion is essentially autosoteric. It contemplates self-salvation. The sinner, therefore, is encouraged to reform. But the Gospel will have none of it. The most thoroughly reformed man in the community, considered by his fellows as a veritable paragon of self-improvement, is met by a blunt "ye must be born again."[11] The Gospel regards the

---

[11]John 3:7.

reformed man as just as far from salvation and Heaven and God as the most abandoned wretch, and calls for the same repentance, the same renunciation of self-trust, the same confession of Christ as Lord, as it requires of the drunkard and the harlot. All this is foreign to the popular idea of man's inherent goodness and divinity.

It is apparent from these considerations that our message is not calculated to make personal evangelism easy. It has in it elements which arouse the fury and the antagonism of the natural man.

D. *Our Adversary.*

While we must not be so taken up with our adversary that we become paralyzed, it will be equally unwise for us to ignore the fact that we have an adversary who will seek to block us at every turn. "We wrestle not against flesh and blood, but against principalities, against powers, against the rulers of the darkness of this world, against spiritual wickedness in high places."[12] The supreme potentate of this great evil, spiritual organization is "your adversary the devil."[13] This is not the place to deal with the doctrine of Satan, but we must not be "ignorant of his devices."[14] One of his favorite devices is to keep us from thinking about him at all, for then we shall not be watchful against him and his practices. But if we insist on spotting him, he will go to the other extreme of tactics, and try so to fill our minds with him that we shall be seized with fear. It will be good for us, then, to take the measure of our enemy, but to balance every remembrance of him with the

---

[12]Eph. 6:12.
[13]I Peter 5:8.
[14]II Cor. 2:11.

assurance that "greater is he that is in you, than he that is in the world."[15]

In his attempts to overturn the work of evangelism, Satan will stir the resentment of the unsaved; he will focus their attention on the unpalatable features of our message so that they will have no eyes for the loveliness of Christ and the blessedness of salvation; he will arouse external opposition, perhaps among relatives or in the social circle; he will create difficult and embarrassing situations; he will draw the attention of the one in whom we are interested to the serious failures of some Christian; and he will by numerous means seek to discourage the soul-winner.

All this is not surprising. We must remember that every attempt to turn a man from his sin to the Saviour is a direct assault on the kingdom of Satan, and we can expect resistance. The resistance seems at times overwhelming. If satanic forces could delay the errand of an angel for twenty-one days,[16] we cannot despise them, nor be surprised if the conflict is at times fierce. But we remember that our adversary has met his superior, and has already been defeated by the cross of Christ. It is our privilege to take victory ground, knowing that we are "more than conquerors through him that loved us."[17]

QUESTIONS AND EXERCISES

1. Discuss the statement: personal evangelism is not easy, and never becomes easy.
2. "Every man is his own greatest problem." Evaluate this statement, especially as it applies to the work of personal evangelism.

---

[15]I John 4:4.
[16]Dan. 10:12, 13.
[17]Rom. 8:37.

3. What is there about the unconverted which makes leading them to Christ difficult?
4. Show how certain aspects of the Gospel message create a difficulty for the personal worker.
5. Describe the tactics of Satan in blocking the work of the soul-winner.

Rewards of Soul-Winning

BELIEVING THAT A TEXTBOOK, and especially one dealing with such a subject as soul-winning, should inspire and encourage us as well as instruct, I am sure it is not out of order to follow the lesson on the difficulties of personal evangelism with a reminder of the rewards that await those who persevere in this blessed occupation.

A. SHOULD REWARDS BE CONSIDERED?

But should reward enter into our consideration at all? Does not that introduce an element of selfishness? If love is the supreme sanction of personal evangelism, does not that immediately rule out all thought of reward?

Such questions sound very pious, but they are not altogether sound, nor are they supported by the Bible. We read about the great renunciation of Moses, but have we forgotten the incentive that supported him in it? "By faith Moses, when he was come to years, refused to be called the son of Pharaoh's daughter; choosing rather to suffer affliction with the people of God, than to enjoy the pleasures of sin for a season; esteeming the reproach of Christ greater riches than the treasures in Egypt: for he had respect unto the recompense of the reward."[1] A greater than Moses, too, was sustained by the hope of reward. Of our blessed Lord it is written: "Who for the joy that was

---
[1]Heb. 11:24-26.

set before him endured the cross, despising the shame, and
is set down at the right hand of the throne of God.'" If the
apostle of the old covenant, and "the Apostle and High
Priest of our profession, Christ Jesus'" were both enabled
to go through the deep waters of their respective callings
by the promise of what lay before, we shall certainly find
support for our wavering spirits in the rewards which are
held out to us in the fulfillment of the sacred task.

B. SOME REWARDS OF SOUL-WINNING.

Let us remember that rewards are not offered as the
motive, but rather as an incentive. God knows our struggles with the world, the flesh, and the Devil, and He knows
our need of stimulation. The rewards yield that stimulation when we are threatened with discouragement. We
shall look, then, at some of the rewards of soul-winning.

1. *Fellowship with Christ.*

The most immediate reward, and perhaps the most precious of all, is fellowship with Christ. Soul-winning is
the work for which the Lord of glory took upon Him our
flesh, for which He humbled Himself as a servant, and
for which He went all the way to Calvary. He did not
ask our help to form the worlds; He does not engage our
co-operation in bearing along the ages; He does not call
for our aid in sustaining the universe. But He has invited
us into partnership with Himself in the work which has
cost Him most and which is dearest to His heart. And if
we have travail of soul in seeking to bring the lost to Him,
if we suffer in the course of our witnessing, we are but
sharing His passion and travail. Indeed, the greater our
suffering in the execution of this work, the deeper our fellowship with Him.

---

²Heb. 12:2.
³Heb. 3:1.

Besides all this, our engagement in this occupation of witnessing assures us of His abiding presence. Whenever we go at His bidding, He accompanies us. Is not that the promise of the Great Commission? "Go ye therefore . . . and, lo, I am with you alway."[4]

2. Development of Character.

There are some rewards which might be called natural rewards. They flow from the very exercise of the task. One of these is character development. We have seen that the winner of souls must be a man of character. Without holiness of life, the springs will dry up and we shall become unfruitful. Hence, as we engage in witnessing in this definite, purposeful way, we are constantly challenged to a life that will bear scrutiny, a life that will accord with the Gospel which we proclaim, a life that will convince those to whom we witness of the reality of the salvation which we offer to them in Christ's name. So we are driven back upon the Lord ourselves, that by the Word and the Spirit we may be vessels "unto honor, sanctified, and meet for the master's use, and prepared unto every good work."[5] A good way, then, to assure our going on in the way of holiness is to persevere in witnessing.

The work itself is a discipline, and discipline strengthens character. The strong character is not the one to whom everything has come uninvited, but rather the one who has fought every step of the way. An undisciplined man is a weak man. Now personal evangelism involves a constant overcoming of obstacles, a constant wrestling with problems, the utmost exercise of our powers. That in itself means a building of our moral and spiritual fiber.

---

[4] Matt. 28:19, 20.
[5] II Tim. 2:21.

Our contacts are human. In this work we are not dealing with machines, but with men; and we are touching them at the deepest springs of their being, at the point of their greatest need, their fiercest conflicts, their most critical problems. If we are conscientious, we cannot but grow in understanding, in sympathy, in patience. So once again the work itself produces its own rewards.

3. *Development of Talents.*

Similarly there is the reward of developed gifts. We have already affirmed that soul-winning never becomes easy. Nevertheless we grow with practice. We learn to discern men's spiritual condition; we become more apt in applying appropriate Scriptures; we learn the wisdom of silence and the wisdom of speech; we learn not to be sidetracked or thrown off balance.

In the parable of the talents,[6] we see how the men who used the talents entrusted to them increased their number. We know, of course, that the talents referred to in the parable were not skills or abilities, but a certain sum of money. But the same principle applies to what we call talents. Exercise develops them and discovers new skills, which in turn are developed. So the man grows, ever richer in gifts and ever more able to use them. In this respect also the work produces its own reward. Surely this is part of the reason why God has chosen to use us. He could use other instruments if He so desired. As John Milton wrote:

> God doth not need
> Either man's work or His own gifts. Who best
> Bear His mild yoke, they serve Him best. His state
> Is kingly. Thousands at His bidding speed
> And post o'er land and ocean without rest.
> They also serve who only stand and wait.[7]

---

[6]Matt. 25:14-30.
[7]John Milton, *On His Blindness.*

He could use His thousands of angels, and not have to trouble with our weaknesses, but He wants to develop us, to bring us to full growth, to "the measure of the stature of the fullness of Christ,"[8] and this is one of His all-wise methods—giving us a work to do that challenges all that is in us.

4. *Joy Unspeakable.*

Of a different order is the reward of unexcelled joy, and yet it also comes with the work.

a) We have suggested that sorrow and travail are associated with the ministry of soul-winning. These are the birth-pangs of spiritual parenthood, and just as in the natural sphere a woman forgets the pain "for joy that a man is born into the world,"[9] so one who has travailed over a soul experiences an ineffable joy in seeing that soul emerge from darkness into light. It is not the joy of statistical success, but the joy of participation in new life. This joy never palls. Its wonder never dims. Sometimes it is more exuberant, more overwhelming, than at other times, and such occasions leave an indelible impression on the memory.

I think, for instance, of an elderly German who lived a rough life in the Northern Ontario bush. His English was poor, his mind undeveloped, and his life one of very narrow limits. His countenance was dark and hard. But the Spirit of God stirred in his soul a sense of need, and he found his way to our services. One Sunday evening I took him into a little side room and tried to present the way of salvation. He did not seem to understand, and I almost despaired of his coming into the light. Finally I suggested that we kneel down and pray. I prayed that God would give light to the darkened

---

[8]Eph. 4:13.
[9]John 16:21.

mind. When we lifted our heads and arose from our
knees, I saw something that startled me, and which I
shall never forget. The darkness and the hardness had
completely fallen away from my friend's countenance. Instead, his face was lit up with a heavenly glow, like a
sunburst. His limited vocabulary made it impossible for
him to say much, but his face spoke volumes. The presence of the Lord in that little room was so real, and the
joy was unspeakable.

b) The joy of parenthood does not end with the birth
of the child. Neither does the joy of the soul-winner end
with the conversion of the sinner. As the passion for souls
is not limited to the desire to see sinners converted but
yearns over the saints to see them conformed to the image
of Christ, so the joy of seeing men born into the family
of God is matched by the joy of witnessing their growth
in the Christian life. Indeed it is in this that one's joy is
fulfilled. Without it the first joy would turn to grief.
John the apostle declared, "I have no greater joy than to
hear that my children walk in truth."[10] Of course he is
speaking here of his spiritual children, his children in the
faith, as the preceding verse makes clear.

One summer when I was at Canadian Keswick, I was
standing on a rock near the hotel, enjoying the magnificent
Muskoka scene. Several bright-faced, happy young people clambered agilely up beside me. One said, "I am one
whom you led to Christ in Stratford." Another broke in,
"And I am another," and a third, "And I am another."
They were all members of one family. It was a true case
of household salvation, and here they were, some years
later, glowing, consecrated Christians, recalling the happy
day. Need I tell you what joy surged through my soul?

---

[10] III John 4.

Or when one receives letters from his "children" who are occupying evangelical pulpits, or ministering in fields afar, or maintaining a clear testimony in a dark place, what joy it brings!

5. *Lasting Friendships Formed.*

The soul-winner's life is enriched with abiding friendships. True Christians do not forget those who led them to the Saviour. In my own case, many influences combined to bring me to the Lord Jesus, but the one whom the Lord used as the final link in the chain was B. McCall Barbour, of Edinburgh, Scotland, who was visiting speaker(the evening of the great decision) at a boys' Bible class which I attended in Alloa. That event in my life started a friendship between him and me which endured as long as he lived. Some of his letters to me are among my most cherished possessions, and when I visited Edinburgh a few years ago, one of the sweetest, most solemn experiences was to stand before his grave and read, with deep emotion, this inscription:

> Benjamin McCall Barbour
> 1864–1943
> Bible Teacher, Writer, Boys' Friend

It was this last phrase that so moved me, for he was that to me.

These happy friendships frequently endure into the second generation. Some time ago we had as guests in our home for a week two lovely Christian young women from Canada. The reason for their visit traces back to the time when I was privileged to lead their mother, then but a young girl, to the Lord. My wife and I are aunt and uncle to that whole family, all rejoicing Christians. I have happy correspondence, too, with a talented young man whose parents I had the joy of pointing to the Saviour before he was born. These friendships are precious beyond rubies.

6. *Approval Bestowed.*

All the rewards mentioned so far have special reference to this present life, although they will all be brought to full fruition in Heaven. There are some rewards, however, which are laid up for us in glory. Our Master has a "Well done!" for all who faithfully served, and that word from Him will surely be reward enough, more than compensating for the travail, the struggle, the disappointments, the discipline, the antagonism which we experienced in the exercise of our high calling. The plaudits of men are shallow and meaningless in comparison.

But the Lord's "Well done!" is not merely a verbal acknowledgment. He accompanies it with substantial expressions of His favor and pleasure. The lord of the parable says: "Thou hast been faithful over a few things, I will make thee ruler over many things."[11] While we do not wish to press the details of the parable, I am sure that our Lord here indicates a place of trust in the everlasting kingdom for those who diligently minister their "talents" here.

In the Epistle to the Hebrews, the Lord Jesus is depicted as surrounded by the hosts of the redeemed, and saying: "Behold, I and the children which God hath given me."[12] It seems to me that such a privilege will be granted the soul-winner in his own measure as he stands before the throne. At least the apostle Paul expected such a reward, for he writes to the Thessalonians: "For what is our hope, or joy, or crown of rejoicing? Are not even ye in the presence of our Lord Jesus Christ at his coming?"[13] Surely the joy of such an occasion will be overwhelming!

Then, by way of final assurance, we have this from Daniel: "They that be wise shall shine as the brightness of the firma-

[11]Matt. 25:21.
[12]Heb. 2:13.
[13]I Thess. 2:19.

ment, and they that turn many to righteousness as the stars forever and ever."[14] The stars in the firmament of sport and entertainment glitter for a little while, then fade into eternal eclipse, but the servants of the Gospel receive an everlasting glory.[15]

QUESTIONS AND EXERCISES

1. Is the thought of rewards a legitimate incentive in the work of soul-winning? Discuss this question.
2. In what senses does the work of soul-winning bring us into fellowship with Christ?
3. How is character developed in the practice of personal evangelism? In what other ways does this work make for development in us?
4. Compare the joy of soul-winning with the joy of parenthood. Enlarge upon this theme.
5. Can you recall, within your own experience or observation, cases of abiding friendships growing out of soul-winning?
6. Search out as many rewards as you can find in the Bible, promised in the time to come to those who win souls. Give references.

---

[14] Dan. 12:3.
[15] I Cor. 9:25

LESSON 11

Preparing for Personal Evangelism

WHEN I CAME into a personal relationship with Christ at
the tender age of nine, I immediately tried to win
others. I have clear recollection of dealing with my play-
mate, and stubbornly holding him at the back door of his
home until he consented to receive the Lord Jesus too. I admit that I had little preparation for that encounter. Shall
we conclude from such experiences that no preparation is
needed for the work of personal evangelism? If one is content to do it always on the basis of a nine-year-old child,
perhaps so. But if we wish to be workmen approved, we
shall seek thorough preparation—not before we ever begin,
but while we are at it, striving to be ever more proficient.

A. STUDY THE WORD OF GOD.

This is basic and of supreme importance.
1. *For Our Own Soul's Nourishment and Sanctification.*
If we remember that the soul-winner must be a man of
character, and the kind of character which the soul-winner
must be, we shall ever be turning to the Book which directs
us in the pursuit of such character. Is not the Word the
water of washing by which Christ sanctifies and cleanses His
Church?[1] We remember how Paul speaks to Timothy about
the inspired Scriptures, affirming that they are "able to make
thee wise unto salvation," and that they are "profitable for

---
[1]Eph. 5:26.

104

doctrine, for reproof, for correction, for instruction in righteousness: that the man of God may be perfect, throughly furnished unto all good works."[2] We shall not very successfully apply the Word of God to the needs of others if we are not well practiced in applying it to our own needs. One who is neglecting the Word of God in his own personal life is incapacitating himself with respect to effectual soul-winning.

2. *So That We May Better Understand the Gospel—Our Duty and Privilege to Present.*

It is because of this point that we gave a whole lesson to "The Message of Evangelism." But let it not be thought that that one lesson exhausted the content of the Gospel! Someone may say, "I believe in the simple Gospel, and that does not need much study or learning." It is true that what we generally present to sinners is "the simple Gospel." We reduce the mighty scheme of redemption to its simplest terms to put it within reach of the mind unaccustomed to the things of God. But anyone who is content to abide in the first simplicities of the Gospel is not growing much, and very soon his witnessing will be a matter of a few hackneyed phrases that have less and less meaning for himself, and not much for those to whom he parrots them. The Gospel is a vast theme, worthy of our best study, and as we enlarge our own apprehension of its glorious truths, we shall be better fitted to present it in its various aspects according to the need of the hour.

Besides, there are so many misconceptions abroad that we must have sufficient understanding of the Gospel to apply corrective measures. These misconceptions range from an extreme legalistic view on the one side to a very shallow "believism" on the other side. We ought to arm ourselves against these with a clear understanding of the doctrine of

---

[2]II Tim. 3:15-17.

grace and a correct view of saving faith. Otherwise we shall be leaving people in bondage, or with false hopes.

3. *That We May Observe the Soul-Winning Methods Described Therein.*

There is no better textbook on soul-winning than the Bible. All we can hope to do in a formal course is to arrange some of the vast amount of Biblical material in systematized form, but this will never take the place of the Bible itself, with the Holy Spirit as teacher. Especially should we examine the work of our Lord and of the apostles in their dealings with individuals. In a later lesson we shall take up a few of the incidents which are particularly helpful in this sphere, but the student should regard these only as examples.

4. *To Have Appropriate Scriptures Ready For Use.*

The great variety of problems which we shall face in the work of soul-winning require them and involve memorization. Memorizing Scripture effectively cannot be accomplished by occasional spurts, but is a matter of consistent, dogged keeping at it, and continual review. The card system is as good as any I know. I suggest that one seeking to engage in this work secure a supply of small cards with a hole punched near one end, and a key ring on which to carry them. He should not attempt to memorize many verses at a time. Begin with one, writing the text on one side of the card and the reference on the other side. Put this card on your key ring, learn it with complete accuracy and until the reference and the text are so married in your mind that you cannot think of the one without the other. When you have so learned one text, engage in the same process with a second. Now you have two texts on your ring. You do not neglect the first, but you continually review it so that the new one will not crowd out the old one. When these two are memorized so that there is no confusion and no mistakes in the reciting, you are ready for a third, and so on.

The question is, What texts will you learn? Later lessons will take up the various types with whom you will have to deal. Begin with one verse that is suggested in connection with the first group of people, then one of the texts suggested for the second group of people, and so on until you have on your ring, and in your mind and heart, one verse for each of the types described. This being done, get a second verse for the first type, and a second verse for the second type, and so on through the list. If you are ambitious you may go through a third time, thus adding to your store. It is wonderful how many verses, with their references, you will have at command in a short time: but keep in mind these principles: (1) do not attempt more than one verse at a time; (2) learn each one thoroughly before proceeding to the next; (3) keep reviewing.[3]

B. STUDY THE OBJECTIONS OF SINNERS.

No branch of an army is more important than the intelligence service, whose duty is to find out all it can about the enemy—his manpower and how it is deployed, the extent and whereabouts of his supplies, his defenses and his plans for offense. What resistance to assault can he muster at this point and that? What plans does he have for aggressive action? Everything which can be known in all these spheres is of priceless value.

If we, then, are going to assail the ramparts of the human soul for Christ, we had better have our intelligence service

---

[3]For the sake of others besides my own students, I would just mention that my plan with the class is to give one verse and reference for each class meeting. I find this is as much as the average class can take, but at every test they are responsible for all the verses that have been given up to that time, so that constant reviewing is assured.—J.C.M.

in operation, to know what resistance we are likely to meet. Only then can we have the appropriate weapons in readiness.

1. *The Method of the Apostle Paul.*

Have you noticed how Paul the apostle anticipated objections to his doctrines of grace, and prepared his artillery against them? We shall mention only a few as samples:

a) The apostle has been arguing that Jews who break the law are rejected, while Gentiles who keep the righteousness of the law are accepted, for it is not a mark in the flesh which makes a true Jew, but a contrite and humble heart. Then he anticipates the objection that in such case the Jew has no advantage, and he answers by showing that their being entrusted with the Holy Scriptures has given them a place of great advantage.[4]

b) Again, he has shown that whatever man does, God shall be vindicated. Even our unrighteousness will turn to the glory of God, for He will be found just and true in His judgments. Immediately the apostle foresees an objection: "Then God is unrighteous to condemn men whose acts only add to the luster of His righteousness. Is it not after all a good thing to sin, seeing that good will come from it— the good of God being justified?" The apostolic answer is satisfied with reminding us that actually it is in the judgment of sin, not in the mere contrast between man's sin and God's goodness, that God is vindicated and glorified. If God did not judge sin, He Himself would stand condemned. This, of course, is unthinkable.[5]

c) In his great declaration of salvation by grace, Paul rises to a climax in the statement: "Where sin abounded, grace did much more abound." He sees that the natural

---

[4]Rom. 2:25–3:2.
[5]Rom. 3:4-8.

heart will raise an objection to that, so he introduces it in the form of a question: "Shall we continue in sin that grace may abound?"[6] The answer is given in the succeeding verses, which reveal that grace is not license to sin, since by the cross we are made dead to sin.

d) A similar problem arises in connection with Paul's doctrine of our emancipation from the bondage of the law. "We are not under the law, but under grace," he exclaims. In full expectation that such a position will be challenged, he himself raises the objection in the form of a question: "What then? shall we sin, because we are not under the law, but under grace?" The answer is interesting. Paul declares that the issue rests on the question of whose servants we are. The servants of sin will go on sinning. The servants of righteousness practice righteousness. Since, then, we have been emancipated from the bonds of sin, we no longer serve sin, but have been bound over to a higher, nobler service, that of righteousness.[7]

The apostle answers other anticipated objections to his teaching concerning the place of the law in the history of sin,[8] his doctrine of sovereign election,[9] and his statements concerning the unbelief of Israel.[10] For our present purpose, however, we are not so much concerned with Paul's answers to specific questions, as with the principle of anticipating objections and having answers ready. He has given us an example in this respect. We ought, therefore, to arm ourselves with arrows in our quiver for every foreseeable occasion.

2. *The Bible Has the Answers.*

---

[6]Rom. 5:20; 6:1.
[7]Rom. 6:14-22.
[8]Rom. 7:7.
[9]Rom. 9:14-24.
[10]Rom. 11:1-5.

We need hardly say, except for emphasis, that the best answer is the Word of God. Most people, even unbelievers, have a respect for the Bible, and what it says carries more weight than any argument which we can muster. But what about the objector who keeps firing back, "You are quoting the Bible, and I don't believe the Bible"? It is not man's belief or unbelief that makes the Word of God "quick, and powerful, and sharper than any two-edged sword."[11] It is that because it is the Word of God, and will pierce the unbelief of the objector more effectively than human persuasion. So, in any case, an answer from God is always best. That means, then, that as we study the objections of sinners, we bring them to the Holy Scriptures for reply.

C. STUDY THE WORK OF OTHER SOUL-WINNERS.

1. *To Keep the Fire Burning.*

There is so much in this world to cool our ardor, in addition to the natural inconsistency of our own heart, that we need all the stimulus and encouragement available. The Holy Spirit uses the Scriptures to this end, but He also uses the experiences of others. To read of their conflicts and conquests, their determination and their successes, often revives our flagging spirit. I doubt if a true child of God can read a report of soul-winning without stirrings of heart. Sometimes there will be self-judgment for neglected opportunities, sometimes a longing for a deeper and truer passion for souls, sometimes an incentive to more diligent application. In some way the fire will burn more brightly, more warmly.

2. *To Improve Our Technique.*

None of us has attained yet to the ultimate of efficiency in this work. What others have done, what approaches

[11] Heb. 4:12.

they have used, how they have applied the Scriptures to new and difficult situations, the errors in methods which they have discovered and corrected—these are all items of importance to every seeker after souls. Admittedly method is not the factor of first importance, but it is important, and can play a large part in determining our success or failure.

The literature in this field is so vast that an exhaustive bibliography would be impractical if it were available. Of more value to the student is a careful selection of books that will provide both inspiration and practical help. Such a selection I have attempted to give in the Bibliography.

D. STUDY THE FALSE CULTS.

False cults are so multiplied today that to master them all would exhaust a lifetime, and prove to be of limited value. However, with a thorough grounding in the Gospel and the teachings of the Holy Scripture, one can very quickly discern the basic errors of the spurious religious systems which abound. While each has its own distinctive features, there are fundamental fallacies in them all. There are also features common to groups of them enabling one to classify them. In most cases, the errors of modern cults are not new, but old ones revived.

These facts make it unnecessary for the average soul-winner to spend too much time delving into the cults, time which could be more profitably spent in active witnessing. It may be required of some to make such study a special ministry in order to put into the hands of Christians in general a concise definition of the errors met with. This will arm the soul-winner with a knowledge of those features in the more common cults which are contrary to the Gospel, and enable him to bring the Scripture [of truth] to bear on these specific

errors. A work which in my opinion does this very effectively is *The Chaos of Cults*, by J. K. VanBaalen.[12]
A later lesson deals with the false cults.[13]

E. SPEND MUCH TIME IN PRAYER.

No preparation is complete without *much prayer*.

1. *Prayer To Keep the Heart In Tune*.

Without prayer, difficulties rooted in ourselves—our lukewarmness, our spasmodic disposition, our unpreparedness,
our fear, our thoughtlessness or our overcaution—will become
insuperable, and we shall find ourselves totally unfitted for
the sacred task. But prayer will maintain contact with those
divine resources which keep us in readiness, "strengthened
with might by his Spirit in the inner man."[14] Vigilance in
prayer will fortify us aganist temptation to indulgences
which weaken the fiber of the soul and make us unfit for
high endeavor.

2. *Prayer Is Part—a Large Part—of Our Warfare Against the Powers of Darkness.*

The apostle Paul, after describing the items of our armor
in the fight against forces of evil, adds this as a necessary
complement, "praying always with all prayer and supplication in the Spirit, and watching thereunto with all perse-
verance."[15] The emphasis here indicates the importance of
prayer in this spiritual warfare, for, as we have already seen,
soul-winning is a warfare.

We have a remarkable example of spiritual triumph
through prayer in the life of Daniel. As he went to prayer,
he was conscious of a deep depression of spirit, which caused

---

[12]J. K. Van Baalen, *The Chaos of Cults* (Grand Rapids: Eerdmans Publishing Co.)
[13]Lesson 21.
[14]Eph. 3:16.
[15]Eph. 6:18.

him to continue in prayer, wrestling in sorrow and perplexity for three weeks, during which time he sustained life by the plainest and most meager diet. As he says: "I ate no pleasant bread, neither came flesh nor wine in my mouth, neither did I anoint myself at all." At the end of the three weeks he was physically exhausted and emaciated, but he had prayed through to victory and was only then acquainted with the nature of the conflict which had been so intense in his own soul. The powers of darkness, represented by a spirit being described as "the prince of the kingdom of Perisa," had fought the angel sent to minister divine truth to Daniel, until Michael came to his assistance.[16] It is a mysterious passage, but it indicates the reality of spiritual warfare and the place of prayer in that warfare. The hosts of Hell are interested in this work of soul-winning, to oppose it with all the power and cunning at their command. Our only answer is prayer, what John Bunyan calls the weapon of All-prayer.

3. *Prayer Secures the Guidance of the Holy Spirit.*

This is a necessary provision in personal evangelism. Many have been brought into real bondage in the matter of witnessing to others, believing that they should deal with all whom they meet regarding the salvation of their soul, and being terribly discouraged when they failed to do so. Now it is true that we must regard all whom we meet as potential recipients of our witness, but not apart from the leading of the Holy Spirit. Bishop Taylor Smith's counsel to soul-winners was that they should never speak unless the Holy Spirit opened the way naturally.[17] Such leading is the privilege of every Christian, but it is the portion only of those who immerse their daily life in prayer.

----

[16]Dan. 10:1-13.
[17]E. L. Langston, *Bishop Taylor Smith* (London: Marshall Morgan and Scott), p. 46.

4. *Prayer Assures the Activity of the Holy Spirit in the Heart of the One Approached.*

We must remember always that it is not our wise approach, or our skillful instruction, or our earnest appeals that will win men to Christ. Important as all these are, they are but the highway of the Holy Spirit's approach. "Not by might, nor by power, but by my spirit, saith the Lord of hosts."[18] The account of the conversion of Lydia is given in these words: "whose heart the Lord opened."[19] Now the Lord works in answer to prayer. We are just as true evangelists when we are praying for the souls of men as when we declare the Gospel to them. And it is certain that we are not as liable to false steps in praying for men as in speaking to men. Moreover, we should make fewer false steps if we prayed more and knew more of the Spirit's workings in men's hearts. This is the primary emphasis in L. S. Chafer's great work, *True Evangelism*,[20] which should be read by all who desire to be winners of souls.

Here, then, are four good reasons for making prayer a large part of our preparation for soul-winning: to keep our own hearts in tune, to wage effective warfare against the adversary, to secure the guidance of the Holy Spirit, and to know the co-operating work of the Holy Spirit in the hearts of those to whom we witness.

QUESTIONS AND EXERCISES

1. If a new Christian can win others to Christ, why is it necessary to undergo a long course of study to prepare for soul-winning? Discuss this question.
2. How will a study of the Bible help us in soul-winning, and what should we specially look for in such a study?

---

[18]Zech. 4:6.
[19]Acts 16:14.
[20]L. S. Chafer, *True Evangelism* (Findlay, Ohio: Dunham Co.).

3. List several of the objections which Paul realized beforehand would be raised to his teaching, and indicate what answers he prepared for those objections. What lesson has this for soul-winners?

4. What are the values of studying the work of other soul-winners?

5. How does prayer prepare us for the work of personal evangelism?

LESSON 12

The Approach

IN THE ACTUAL OPERATION of personal evangelism, there are four steps—the approach, the instruction, the appeal, and the follow-up. That is the order, and any attempt to reverse it will end in catastrophe.

A. IMPORTANCE OF RIGHT APPROACH.

The approach is tremendously important, because first impressions count, for good or ill. A wrong approach is likely to arouse resentment and predispose the one so approached to determined resistance, while a proper approach may prove completely disarming. Even one who is sympathetic and has a heart hunger for God will shy away from a crude approach, while one who tends toward antagonism is frequently won over by a gracious word.

1. *The Right Mental Attitude.*

The battle of the approach must be won on the field of one's own mental attitude. To begin with, we must rid our minds of any sense of superiority. If that exists, it cannot be hidden, and we are defeated before we begin. No man is going to accept our superiority, not even the derelict on Skid Row. Evangeline Booth looked for something in which she could affirm that the people with whom she dealt were ahead of her—even if it were only in the knowledge of sin![1] The "holier than thou" attitude is fatal to soul-winning. As

[1]*The Reader's Digest,* August, 1947.

116

for the "wiser than thou" attitude, that belongs to the unbeliever. Let him have it. "God hath chosen the foolish things of the world to confound the wise."[2] By the same token, we must avoid a false, sentimental pity. Our attitude must be neither, "You old sinner," nor "You poor sinner!" We must see men as souls for whom Christ died, and yearn over them with a solicitude void of superiority.

On the other hand, a sense of inferiority will kill our efforts. If we quail before men's superior position, or superior learning, or superior ability, we shall greatly weaken our witness. We want to remember the words of Hezekiah: "With him is an arm of flesh; but with us is the Lord our God to help us."[3]

2. *The Right Qualities.*

This matter of approach cannot be reduced to mechanics or an algebraic formula. It is a matter of the heart, and the more natural, the better. The studied approach can so easily degenerate into something professional and formal, and lose the appeal of the spontaneous. Nevertheless, there are some qualities which everyone ought to cultivate, especially if he has a tendency to the opposite.

a) For instance, the approach must always be courteous. In an automobile establishment to which I take my car for repairs a motto hangs: "We are never too busy to be courteous." I have never known them to belie that slogan. If business concerns demand courtesy of their representatives in their contacts with the public, how much more should we who represent the God of all grace show courtesy at all times, and especially when we are engaged in His business? This was a marked feature in our Lord's dealing with individuals. Consider the case of the woman at Sychar's well,

[2] I Cor. 1:27.
[3] II Chron. 32:8.

whom the rabbis would utterly have spurned on three counts
—that she was a woman, and a sinner, and a Samaritan. But
see with what refinement and grace our Lord spoke to her,
beginning with a request for a drink of water, and leading
her step by step into the knowledge of Himself.[4]

The apostle Paul also preserved proper decorum of speech,
and addressed men in the terms of courtesy befitting their
position, while never mincing his message through respect
of persons.

b) The approach must be made tactfully as well as
courteously. Tact means touch. If a doctor has a coarse
touch or an uncertain touch, he instills fear in the patient,
but if he has a touch at once gentle and confident, he in-
spires assurance, and quiets fear. Now we readily admit
that one can make a fetish of tact and become so tactful
that he never makes contact. There may be occasions when
the best tact is in being completely frank and straightforward, so long as there is no sting or barb in our hook. A
good example of this straightforward tact was seen in the
conversion of the Scottish attorney, Gordon Forlong, in
1851.

In that year this noted lawyer, whose textbook, *Epitome
of Scottish Law,* was a standard for many years, but whose
attitude to Christianity was one of antagonism, went to
London to establish a Bank of Character and Skill similar
to the one he had organized in Scotland. Among others to
whom he applied for assistance in this charitable work was
Mr. George Hitchcock, a London merchant and a Christian,
who listened carefully to the young Scotsman's story and
responded with a substantial gift. As he handed the check
to the delighted pleader, Mr. Hitchcock said quietly, "What
a pity, Mr. Forlong, that you are not a Christian!" The

[4]John 4.

shocked lawyer made some attempt at self-defense, but found himself void of a case, and agreed to read a little book which Mr. Hitchcock gave him, *The Philosophy of the Plan of Salvation.* This he did as he sailed back to Edinburgh in a coastal vessel. By the time he reached home he was a rejoicing believer. Thereafter his passion was to make Christ known, in which task he spent his remaining thirty-eight years, being mightily used in Edinburgh, then in London, and finally for twenty years in New Zealand.[5]

Tact, then, is not "pulling your punches," but it is making the contact in the most effective manner. To do this, we shall have to seek that "wisdom that is from above,"[6] which God promises to those who ask[7] as the portion of those who are filled with the Holy Spirit.[8]

c) Wisdom should be used with regard to the *when* of our approach as well as the *how* of it. To embarrass a person in the presence of another is only to prejudice the situation. We cannot always wait till we find the object of our concern all alone, but we should do our best to separate him from others before we broach these matters. This is especially necessary if the third party is unsympathetic and cynical. We remember how the apostle Paul was up against this difficulty in speaking to Sergius Paulus of Cyprus, although he was summoned for that very purpose, so that he was under the necessity of silencing Elymas the sorcerer before he could proceed successfully with his witness.[9] I have known mothers who played an effective game of interference when their boys were being spoken to and were

---

[5]This information was gleaned from an editorial in the *Sunday School Times* of December 27, 1941, based on *Memorial Notes from Gordon Forlong,* by his daughter.
[6]James 3:17.
[7]James 1:5.
[8]Acts 6:3.
[9]Acts 13:6, 12.

manifesting real interest. Their most devastating interference was usually their insistence that "Tom is a good boy," when I was trying to show Tom from the Word of God that he was a sinner!

B. TYPES OF RIGHT APPROACH.

The approach can, in general, be divided into two types, the direct and the indirect. These scarcely need definition. The direct approach comes immediately to the central question, while the indirect leads to it by a more circuitous route. Both methods have their virtues and their dangers. The direct approach frequently shocks the sinner into an aroused interest, while sometimes it repels him and induces him to retire from the scene. The indirect approach is calculated to win confidence and arouse a more lasting interest, but its danger is to become lost before it reaches the goal.

1. *Indirect Type.*

An outstanding champion of the indirect approach was H. Clay Trumbull, whose son, Charles, organized and presented his father's principles and methods in an excellent work, *Taking Men Alive.*[10] The elder Trumbull believed that winning a man to oneself was a necessary step in leading him to Christ. It is certainly true that if a man is suspicious of us, or prejudiced against us, we stand a sorry chance of helping him. We must win his confidence. The two methods suggested by Mr. Trumbull are commendation and common interest.

Commending sinners may seem like precarious business and certainly calls for care. The commendation must be sincere and honest, else it will lack the approval of the Holy Spirit, and the sinner himself will discern the hypocrisy. Mr. Trumbull tells of a friend of his who started a conver-

---

[10]Charles G. Trumbull, *Taking Men Alive* (New York: Association Press), p. 75.

sation with an old colored stone-breaker by telling him that
he was doing a good piece of work—the first time in twenty
years, as the old man affirmed, that anybody had given him
such encouragement.[11] Condemnation will put one on the
defensive, but sincere commendation, especially where it
has been little known, will more often prepare a heart for a
true confession of sin.

Common interests often create a bond which makes frank
and sincere conversation easier. Discovering that you both
come from the same part of this or another country, that
you both play golf or use the rod, that you both read poetry
or are radio hams, can be an opening wedge. Or if you fail
to find common interests, make yourself interested in the
other fellow's interests. Mr. Trumbull tells of George Williams'[12] plan for winning a braggart infidel named Rogers,
who was furiously persecuting the Christians in the business
house where he held a responsible position. Discovering that
Rogers had a passion for oysters, Williams suggested an
oyster supper, to which Rogers was to be invited, but at
which no attempt at his conversion was to be made. The
persecutor, amused at the "frivolity" of the Christians, took
the invitation as a dare, and accepted. The behavior of the
group deeply affected him, and he was brought under such
conviction of sin that after several days he sought out the
Christians and became one of them.

2. *Direct Type*.

The direct approach is well represented by such men as
Hebich of India, and Dad Hall, the "Bishop of Wall Street."
An illustration of Hebich's direct approach is his dealing
with a certain major of the British engineers in India. Seeing
Hebich approaching his bungalow, the major told his servant

---

[11]*Ibid.*, p. 79.
[12]*Ibid.*, p. 104. George Williams (later Sir George Williams) was the
founder of the YMCA, and Rogers was one of the first twelve members.

not to let the "padre" in, but tell him the master was not at home. But Hebich had caught a glimpse of the major, and pushed by the boy into the house. Searching all the rooms of the house, Hebich did not find his man until he returned to the living room and looked under a sofa which had drapery with fringes down to the floor. "Come out, you coward," demanded the missionary. The major obeyed. "Sit down, you coward," was the next command. Again the soldier obeyed. "Hear God's message, you coward." Then Hebich launched into a veritable sermon on hiding from God, citing Adam in the Garden of Eden. Soon the major was on his knees, crying for mercy.[13]

3. *What Factors Determine Approach?*

What factors will determine the type of approach to be used?

a) First, one's own disposition. Saints are no more built on the assembly-line pattern than are sinners. Some of us are so constituted psychologically that we do everything with a direct plunge, while others are careful in the laying of plans. One youth proposes with a blunt, hearty, "Maggie, let's get married." On the other hand, we have heard of the bashful lover who puzzled for weeks over the method of approaching the delicate subject. Finally he hit on a plan. One lovely Saturday afternoon he took his lady-love for a walk—through the cemetery! He led her to the family plot, and told her of all the dear people who lay there—grandparents, great-grandparents, and so on. Then, with great trepidation he added, "Susie, how would you like to lie there?" Now if we transfer these two into the realm of personal evangelism, you will expect that the first would use the direct approach, while the second would be more likely to employ the indirect approach—let us hope with more

---

[13]Alfred Mathieson, *Hebich of India* (Scotland: John Ritchie, Ltd.), p. 60.

wisdom! I can hardly imagine Hebich arranging an oyster supper for these British officers in India, with instructions that the topic of their salvation was not to be introduced; and I can scarcely visualize George Williams forcing his way past a servant into another's house, excoriating him for his wickedness and demanding instant repentance. Disposition will play a large part in this matter.

b) In the second place, the particular situation will somewhat determine the type of approach. How much time is at our disposal? Is death imminent? Is this a casual meeting or a more or less permanent association? Is there evidence of a work of the Holy Spirit begun? Has the person in whom we are interested some knowledge of the things of God, or is he totally ignorant? Have we met in a situation which spontaneously makes men think of God? These and many other questions can be asked of the occasion. Sometimes the repeating of a verse of Scripture is as much as the situation allows, but if the object of our evangelism is a new neighbor, we shall begin by showing kindnesses and letting our light shine.

c) Finally, the approach must be determined by the leading of the Holy Spirit. This calls for a life of walking in the Spirit, for preparedness of heart, for sensitivity to the voice of the Spirit, for spiritual wisdom. The one who is much in the secret place will qualify for this delicate task.

C. SUGGESTED WAYS OF RIGHT APPROACH.

It would be impossible, even if it were in the province of this book, to give an exhaustive list of ways to approach this greatest of all topics. A few examples may stir the student to alertness in the matter.

1. *Current News.*

Frequently the outstanding news of the day may be the

opening wedge. A miscarriage of justice or the inability of
the police department to track down the perpetrator of a
crime offers opportunity to speak of the sure judgments of
God. A catastrophe suggests the greater tragedy of a lost
soul or the need to be ready to meet God. The death of a
prominent person indicates that death is no respecter of
persons, and here Hebrews 9:27 may be applied. A big
sports event may recall the sports passages of the New
Testament. Even a boxing match may draw the comment,
"Did you know that the apostle Paul was a boxer?" Then
refer to I Corinthians 9:27, where the word translated "keep
under" in the King James Version means to bruise, to beat
black and blue. This may lead to a discussion of the spiritual conflict which is raging in every man's soul.

2. *Daily Occupations.*

A conversation of any length between men usually touches
on their several occupations. That may be the point of contact. For teachers, Jesus is the great Teacher; for doctors,
He is the Great Physician for whom no case ever proved too
difficult; for lawyers, He is the great Advocate or *Solicitor*
who has a watertight case on behalf of every client who
applies to Him, and the Judge who has a foolproof case
against every sinner who refuses to repent; for the baker,
He is the Bread from Heaven; for a rancher, He is the Good
Shepherd; for fisherman, He is the Master of the craft, under
whose direction experts who had failed brought in the fish
by the boat load. Remember that these are only "openers."

3. *Public Bible Reading.*

Some object to reading the Bible in a public conveyance,
lest it should seem like Pharisaism. On the other hand, it
may make openings for the Gospel. On the occasion I was
on a long train journey, traveling Pullman. I could not waste
the hours, for I had work to do. I asked for a table and be-

gan writing the lesson article for the *Sunday School Times.*
My Bible was on the table, along with the other equipment.
The presence of that Bible made two passengers stop and
talk, so I had two very profitable conversations as a result
of having my Bible open.

We must be ready, prayerful, and alert.

QUESTIONS AND EXERCISES

1. Why is the approach so important?
2. Discuss the statement: The battle of the approach must be won on the field of one's own mental attitude.
3. What are the characteristics of a good approach?
4. What are the two general types of approach? What are the values and the dangers of each type?
5. By what means did Dr. Trumbull suggest that we gain men's confidence as preparatory to witnessing for Christ?
6. What factors will determine the type of approach used? Explain.
7. Prepare a list of possible approaches to imaginary characters in imaginary situations. (Be realistic, however!) Do not use the examples in the lesson.

LESSON 13

Following Through

THE WORK IS ONLY BEGUN when we have made the approach, although making the approach is often the most difficult part of the work, because it is the part over which we generally have the biggest struggle. There is a tendency with some to be hit-and-run witnesses. They fire a single shot and then run for their lives! The true personal evangelist will want to see the matter through.

A. INSTRUCTION.

After the approach, comes the instruction; that is, where the approach has discovered some interest.

Sometimes the approach is rebuffed, and we are inclined then to become argumentative, or to beat a hasty retreat. Both are wrong. A combative spirit will ruin our chances of doing any good. Even if we win the argument, we are likely to lose the soul we seek to win. Or we may lose both! On the other hand, to give evidence that the rebuff has squelched us will stir in the other little admiration for the Christian or for Christianity. We must stand our ground, even if it be only with a smile. "A soft answer turneth away wrath."[1] Grace and wisdom in such a situation may turn the rebuff into inquiry. At least the rebuff will lose its force, and the friend will have some firsthand evidence of the reality of our Christian faith.

---

[1]Prov. 15:1.

Another mistake is to regard a show of interest as a decision, or at least as the basis for an appeal to make a decision. Instead, interest is nothing more than a basis for instruction. Decisions made without instruction in the way of salvation are apt to be short-lived. Remember the parable of the four soils.[2] The first of the soils mentioned represents those who have no understanding, from whose hearts the seed of the Word is quickly snatched. Our responsibility is to see that men have understanding as well as interest. Hence the need for instruction. Never jump from approach to appeal, however inviting the prospect may be to obtain easy results. The results may turn out to be tragic.

To bypass instruction is dishonest, both toward God and toward men. It may be tedious work, requiring much patience, much repetition, much versatility, but it will pay big dividends in enlightened, stable converts.

1. *Must Be Simple.*

Instruction at this point must be simple, elementary, and based on clear Scriptures. This is not the time to give discourses on the eternal decree, election, the hypostatic union, and such like. These can await a course in Systematic Theology. The matters to make clear are personal sinnerhood. God's provision in Christ, and the need for personal, definite, and immediate acceptance of that provision in repentance and faith. There will always be the temptation to introduce other more advanced themes, especially with people of superior learning, but one must learn to stick to the first principles of the Gospel in dealing with the unsaved.

2. *Must Have No Feeling of Superiority.*

It is important to look to one's own spirit in giving instruction to others. We are all too prone to have a feeling of superiority in such a situation, and that is fatal to the

[2]Matt. 13:18-23.

work of soul-winning. If only we remember that our salvation is all of grace, and all our knowledge of the things of God is of grace, we shall be able to instruct others in a spirit of meekness and humility, with love, and our instructions will not become offensive, but will be gratefully received. Even doctors who give directions to nurses and patients with a superior air are despised. How much more Christians who represent the "meek and lowly" Jesus! This does not mean that there will be no note of authority in our teaching. There will be. But it will be the authority of the truth itself, the authority of the Word of God, not an "air" of authority.

3. *May Use His Own Testimony.*

Personal testimony is quite in order as an aid to the seeker, so long as our testimony exalts the glory and all-sufficiency of Christ as Saviour rather than our character either before or after conversion. We must glory neither in our past sins nor in our present attainment. Above all we must avoid a "holier than thou" attitude. We are only sinners, saved by grace, and we are pointing men to the Savior, not to ourselves as examples of sinners, or as examples of saints. This latter we should be, indeed, for others to see without our calling attention to the fact. So, provided the personal testimony exalts Jesus and helps to clarify some point in the instruction or encourage the seeker, it is a thoroughly legitimate procedure. For instance, if the seeker is experiencing some difficulty with respect to faith that you remember having at the time of your conversion, your relating how the Lord lifted you over the obstacle will be helpful. A Spirit-led worker will know how to use all these instruments.

B. APPEAL.

When the instruction has been given, and a sufficient understanding of the way of salvation is manifested, then,

and not till then, is it time for the appeal. Teaching ought
to issue in action, and action certainly should be enjoined on
one who has received instruction in the way of life. An
evangelist, personal or otherwise, is not only an instructor,
but also a pleader for God, even as Paul said, "Now then we
are ambassadors for Christ, as though God did beseech you
by us: we pray you in Christ's stead, be ye reconciled to
God."[3] If we lose the pleading note, we shall be failing in a
large portion of our task. Instruction, important as it is,
is not conversion, but without the due response will turn
to condemnation. We do not want to leave men in that
sorry state.

1. *Seek Action.*

Let us remember, too, that we are seeking a verdict of
the will, not simply an assent of the intellect. The reason
and the emotions are ultimately only corridors by which
to reach the will. We are aiming at an act of submission
to Christ as Lord, an act of self-committal to Him as Saviour.
Nothing short of that is the goal of the true evangelist.
Therefore, when the intellect has been enlightened in regard to the truth of God, the question must be pressed—
What will you do about it?

2. *Wait for Guidance of Holy Spirit.*

Having said that, however, we must issue a solemn warning against overpressure on the human plane. Insistence
may result in one of two tragedies—a stiffening against the
Gospel even where some interest had been aroused, or a
premature confession which lacks the work of the Holy
Spirit. In either case the latter state is worse than the former.
Unripe fruit will prove to be bitter fruit. Here again, the
personal soul-winner greatly needs to be in full communion
with the Holy Spirit, that he may go along with the Holy

---

[3]II Cor. 5:20.

Spirit instead of running ahead of Him. See how we must be led by the Spirit of God every step of the way.

C. FOLLOW-UP.

The appeal has been made, and let us trust, has met with the response of glad decision for Christ. Is the personal evangelist's work now finished? No! In a sense it has only begun. Do you remember what we said about the passion for souls?[4] It is twofold. It is characterized by an earnest desire to see sinners converted, and an equal concern to see saints perfected. Now then, right before our eyes a sinner has been made a saint. Right away that aspect of our passion for souls which longed for his salvation gives place to that other aspect of our passion for souls which longs for his sanctification. Here is a newborn babe. We want him to grow. Immediately the follow-up begins. From now on our work may not be strictly that of the evangelist, but rather that of the pastor. Even so, it is a work that must be done. How far we should carry it depends on the circumstances of the case.

When we come to specialties in personal evangelism, we shall be dealing with follow-up work in connection with evangelistic campaigns and rescue missions. For the present we shall deal with it only in a general way.

1. _Explanation._

The first thing a young convert needs is an understanding of what has actually taken place, coupled with an assurance of salvation. Here another warning is needed. Never tell one who has just professed faith in Christ that he is saved. Let the Holy Spirit tell him that, through the Word, and then let him tell you. Any assurance which the Christian worker gives will evaporate with the first temptation, but the witness of the Spirit will abide. We, however, may turn

---

4Lesson 8.

the new Christian to the great assurance passages, such as
I John 5:10-13, and let the Holy Spirit speak to him through
them. Then to send him on his way rejoicing, we may show
him from the Scriptures some of the great blessings of
salvation: the putting away of our sins,[5] becoming a child
of God,[6] having the Holy Spirit dwell in our hearts,[7] and
others of like assuring nature. But not too much for a beginning! Remember that he is a babe, and should not be asked
to digest a big steak the day he is born! A good big drink of
"the sincere milk of the word"[8] is as much as he can take.

2. *Counsel*.

Having thus given the new Christian his first "bottle," a
father-in-God is in a position to give some good counsel.
Four exercises should be urged upon the young convert—
Bible reading, prayer, confession, and church attendance.
A truly born-again person will not need much urging in these
matters, but will benefit from some thoughtful guidance.

a) Have you found a good plan of Bible reading? Pass
it along. Better still, supervise the young convert's reading
until he is well launched in that mighty ocean of eternal
truth. It may be that he will want to come to you for help
in the understanding of it. Be ready to help. Perhaps his
questions will show you how much you stand in need of
Bible study yourself! Then study it together, if the situation allows. You might do well to suggest some correspondence courses, such as those offered by some Bible institutes.

b) As for prayer, encourage him to "carry everything to
God in prayer." Remind him that in prayer he should express his heart to God quite freely, and at the same time
learn to be silent before God. The great prayer passages of

---

[5] Ps. 103:12.
[6] I John 3:2.
[7] Rom. 8:9.
[8] I Peter 2:2.

the Bible should be drawn to his attention.[9] The "quiet time" should be urged as a regular daily habit, preferably in the morning, with as many other times of going apart with God as possible.

c) Witnessing is tremendously important in the Christian life, both as a means of spiritual health and as a means of winning others. While public confession is not laid down as a condition of salvation, it is so bound up with salvation as an expression of it that the salvation of those who refuse to confess their faith stands gravely in doubt. A nonconfessing Christian is a contradiction and a travesty. Our Lord offers strong encouragement to open confession of Him, and issues solemn warning against failure to do so.[10] Confession is the outlet which keeps the stream of blessing flowing and saves the believer from becoming a Dead Sea.

d) *Needs a Local Church.*

Another item in the follow-up is to introduce the new Christian to a good local church. This may not always be easy. The convert may live in a community quite unknown to the personal worker, who therefore can make no recommendation. There are, however, some places where inquiry can be made—such as Moody Bible Institute, which has a large mailing list, and is in touch with evangelical churches and ministers over a wide area. Failing this, one must be content to counsel the young believer to seek out a company of Christians where the truth by which he was saved is clearly taught, and to pray that the Holy Spirit will guide him in his search. When we have done all our duty in this respect, we can trust, and not be afraid. After all, we can expect the Great Shepherd to take care of His sheep.

When one knows of a church in which a young believer would be nurtured, it is a gracious gesture to write to the

---

[9] Such as Luke 11:1-13; 18:1-7.
[10] Luke 9:26.

pastor of that church, giving him the name and address of the convert, with a report of the conversion, and requesting that he seek him out. On the other hand, urge the new Christian to introduce himself to the minister. An alert pastor will encourage a babe in Christ, and make opportunities for him to render some service in the church, according to his ability and readiness.

3. *Continued Interest.*

Unless the situation indicates that it would be inappropriate or unwise, one who has led a soul to the Lord will want to maintain personal contact, at least until the young Christian is well established. He will be careful, however, not to intrude on the prerogatives and duties of others, but will stand by as a friend and prayer-helper. The occasional letter, suggestions in good reading, sharing experiences, and in general showing an unflagging interest, will go a long way to help him to "grow in grace, and in the knowledge of our Lord and Saviour Jesus Christ."[11]

QUESTIONS AND EXERCISES

1. What mistakes are frequently made: (a) when the approach meets with a rebuff? (b) when it discovers an interest?
2. What should be the character of the instruction given one who shows interest in the Gospel?
3. Discuss the place of personal testimony in the instruction given to a seeker.
4. Discuss the parts played by the reason, the emotions, and the will in conversion.
5. What dangers must be avoided with respect to the appeal?
6. What spiritual exercises should be urged upon a new convert? Discuss their importance.
7. Why is it important to get a new convert linked with a local church?

---

[11] II Peter 3:18.

Lessons from Gospel of John

IN OUR LESSON on "Preparation for Personal Evangelism" we took note of the necessity for studying the Bible in order to learn how souls were dealt with there. Let us examine three examples from John's Gospel.

A. PERSONAL EVANGELISM IN JOHN 1.

The first chapter of John's Gospel is full of personal evangelism, especially from verse 35 to the end of the chapter.

1. *The Spheres of Witnessing.*

a) The first is the sphere of discipleship.[1] John the Baptist pointed out Jesus to two of his own followers, who immediately went after the Saviour.

b) Following this we see witnessing in the sphere of kinship.[2] Andrew, one of the two who followed Jesus at the instigation of John the Baptist, immediately went after his brother Simon, who later became the leader of the apostolic band.

c) Again, in the circle of friendship the witness was pressed.[3] Philip, who had been found by Jesus Himself, went to his friend Nathanael with the good news, and, bringing him to Jesus, had the joy of hearing him greeted as "an Israelite indeed, in whom is no guile."

---

[1] John 1:36.
[2] V. 41.
[3] V. 45.

This should teach us that every relationship which we may hold with others becomes a sphere of witnessing. All human bonds mean responsibility. If we recognize that these human circles which surround us are not accidents but the orderings of the Lord, we shall be gripped with a sense of purpose regarding them all. They constitute our "territory" as representatives of Christ.

2. *The Characteristics of Witnessing.*

a) First, it was personal. John the Baptist pointed out Jesus as the Lamb of God on two consecutive days. From the context we gather that the first occasion was in the course of his public preaching.[4] The record does not indicate any turning of men to follow Jesus that day. But the following day, when John's audience consisted of only two of his own disciples, his witness concerning the Lamb of God resulted in both of them going after Jesus.[5] All the other cases of witnessing were definitely personal.

b) Again, the witness was purposeful. Within the compass of five verses[6] the verb *to find* is used five times, twice concerning men finding Christ, once concerning Christ finding men, and twice concerning men finding other men. In no case was the finding accidental, but in every case it was the result of seeking. In other words, it was deliberate and purposeful. The men who found Christ were seekers. The Lord Himself was a seeking Saviour. Andrew and Philip were likewise men of purpose who went out to find others with whom they desired to share their great discovery.

c) The witness was also positive. There was no note of doubt in the declaration of any of these men. "Behold the Lamb of God!" exclaimed John.[7] "We have found the

---

[4]John 1:29-31.
[5]Vv. 35-37.
[6]Vv. 41-45.
[7]V. 36.

136

Messias," declared Andrew.[8] And Philip is just as positive: "We have found him, of whom Moses in the law, and the prophets, did write."[9] One is tempted to examine the thinking of these three men from their various ways of referring to the Lord, but this is not the place for such a digression. But we can at least observe that there can be variety in the form of our witnessing.

3. *The Elements in Witnessing.*

a) First there is bold declaration. "Behold the Lamb of God!"[10] If you will, that is dogmatic theology, and we cannot give a true witness without introducing dogmatics. That is of the essence of what Christ meant when He said to His disciples, "Ye shall be witnesses unto me."[11] Peter launched his career of dogmatic theology when he uttered his great confession: "Thou art the Christ, the Son of the living God."[12] His sermon on the Day of Pentecost revealed the dogmatic theologian *par excellence.*[13] This does not mean speaking in dictatorial tones, but it does mean declaring with unquestioning confidence the truth concerning Jesus.

b) We observe in the second place the note of personal testimony. Andrew and Philip both state, "We have found."[14] That is the very essence of personal testimony. If we are going to bear witness to all that Christ is, we must be able to say that we have found Him to be just that, and if our lives confirm our testimony it will be so much more convincing.

c) The third element present in the witness of this chapter is the persuasive invitation.[15] When Nathanael ques-

[8]V. 41.
[9]V. 45.
[10]John 1:36.
[11]Acts 1:8.
[12]Matt. 16:16.
[13]Acts 2:22-24, 36.
[14]Vv. 41, 45.
[15]V. 46.

tioned Philip's testimony with the old prejudice, "Can there
any good thing come out of Nazareth?" Philip did not argue,
but issued a very sensible invitation, "Come and see." Argument has no place in witnessing. It only jeopardizes the
issue and tends to stiffen resistance, but a kindly invitation
to "come and see" disarms opposition.

B. PERSONAL EVANGELISM IN JOHN 3.

We turn next to our Lord's dealing with Nicodemus.[16]
Now Nicodemus was a Pharisee, but he was not of the
number of hypocrites who so largely made up that sect.
Certainly the Lord did not deal with him as a hypocrite,
but treated him as an earnest, sincere seeker. He was
moral, religious, taught in the law, honored by his coreli-
gionists, and esteemed as a teacher. But he was puzzled and
strangely blind. I do not believe that his coming to Jesus
by night should be attributed to cowardice, but rather to
a desire for a longer, less interrupted interview than would
be possible by day, considering the crowds that thronged
Jesus in those earlier days of His ministry.

Our special interest lies in our Lord's dealing with Nicodemus. We can discern a threefold treatment. I like to
call it the "shock" treatment, the "light" treatment, and the
"time" treatment.

1. The "Shock" Treatment.

Notice how the Lord broke in on the pretty, compli-
mentary speech of Nicodemus with "except a man be born
again, he cannot see the kingdom of God."[17] That was
really shock treatment. It was a new thought for this religious leader, and it completely baffled him. Moreover,
Jesus did not immediately help him out of his amazement,

---

[16] John 3:1-21.
[17] V. 3.

but rather increased it, as if to allow the shock to have full effect. Four things Jesus told Nicodemus about being born again—the necessity of it,[18] the means of it,[19] the reason for it,[20] and the mystery of it.[21] This teacher of Israel was really beyond his depth, groping for a straw to which his understanding could cling.

2. *The "Light" Treatment.*

Then Jesus brought on the light treatment, and it is significant that the light focuses upon Himself, Son of man and only begotten Son of God. It was light concerning the way of life. He had been speaking about the way of life as a miracle of God in the new birth. He now brings it down to the human level, where man must take hold of it.

There were three rays to this light treatment, three simple facts which make plain the way of life.

a) Life is through the Son of man.[22] There is no ascending up to Heaven apart from Him who came down from Heaven. His descending was for the very purpose of taking sinners with Him in His ascending.

b) Life is through the Son of man lifted up.[23] Now the lifting up mentioned here clearly points to the cross, of which the serpent in the wilderness was a picture. But the lifting up was not exhausted on the cross. That was the beginning of the lifting up, and the sacrificial and suffering part of it. The end of the lifting up is the throne, the Father's right hand. It is not a Jesus hanging on a cross who draws all men to Him,[24] but the Jesus who, having once for all put away sin by the sacrifice of Himself,[25] now

[18]V. 3.
[19]V. 5.
[20]V. 6.
[21]V. 8.
[22]John 3:13.
[23]V. 14.
[24]John 12:32.
[25]Heb. 7:27.

lives, exercising an all-sufficient saviourhood based on that sacrifice.

c) Life is through faith in the Son of man.[26] The redemptive work of Christ calls for the response of faith, trust, acceptance. Just as the presence of the brazen serpent in the midst of the camp of stricken Israel did not heal the victims of the scourge without that look of faith, so neither does the lifting up of Christ save a soul without the appropriate response of faith. It must be so if God is going to treat us as moral agents, as men endowed with the faculty of choice, and not as automatons.

Do you see how simple is the way of salvation as man is asked to grasp it, although it is so baffling and inscrutable as God has to perform it?

3. *The "Time" Treatment.*

Now what do we mean by the time treatment? Just this, that our Lord did not press Nicodemus for an immediate verdict and confession. I am not saying that we should never press for immediate decisions, but when we do, we want to be sure that we have the permission and the leading of the Holy Spirit in doing so. More and more I am struck with the absence of such pressure methods in the ministry of our Lord. Here, in the case of Nicodemus, He gave him the shock that mystified him and the light which illumined him, and then he handed him over to time *and the Holy Spirit.* He was not impatient for hasty, unripe decisions, because He believed in the ministry of the Holy Spirit. We profess to believe in the Holy Spirit, but too often our actions indicate that we believe in ourselves far more. At any rate, we do not believe that the Holy Spirit of God can work apart from us and our immediate presence!

The time treatment worked. We have two further notices

---

[26]Vv. 15, 16.

about Nicodemus in John's Gospel.[27] In both he is seen
standing for Jesus. Some do not think that he stood very
heroically before the Sanhedrin, but he stood, and he stood
alone! Then when all had fled, Nicodemus joined hands
with Joseph of Arimathaea in saving Jesus from the burial
of a criminal. He proved himself a friend of Jesus, for he
had found a Friend in Jesus.

C. PERSONAL EVANGELISM IN JOHN 4.

Our third example is from the story of the Samaritan
woman whom our Lord met at Jacob's well outside the village of Sychar.[28] Here was a situation in which there were
barriers to be broken down—quite different from the case
of Nicodemus.

1. *Barriers.*

We can see three barriers—the sex barrier, the race barrier,
and the moral barrier. It was contrary to rabbinical custom
to instruct a woman. The Jews had no dealings with the
Samaritans.[29] Religious leaders shunned the company of
sinners. But Jesus, the rabbi, taught this woman; Jesus, the
Jew, treated this Samaritan on a footing of equality; Jesus,
the religious leader, dealt with this sinner to save her from
her sin. Not often shall we have to break through so many
barriers in a single situation, but frequently there will be
some barrier to overcome that will call for grace and wisdom beyond that which we have by nature.

Our Lord's method with the woman of Samaria is full
of instruction for us.

2. *Approach.*

Look at the approach first. It was the indirect approach.
Jesus was weary and thirsty, sitting on the well. The woman

[27]John 7:50; 19:39.
[28]John 4:1-30.
[29]V. 9.

also was thirsty, but with another thirst. While Jesus needed some of the water of the well to slake a physical thirst, she needed the water of life which only He could give to satisfy her soul's deepest longings. The Lord's supreme desire was to give this woman what she needed, but He made His own need the means of approach. His request for a drink[30] was indeed startling, considering the barriers just enumerated. Indeed, it was sufficiently startling to arouse the woman's interest immediately. This was no ordinary Jew whom she had met. His request prepared her for the truth that He had to reveal to her.

3. *Instruction.*

I think the instruction finds its focal point in verses 13 and 14 where a palpable truth is linked with a promising proposition: "Whosoever drinketh of this water shall thirst again." She certainly knew the truth of that. But Jesus did not stop there: "But whosoever drinketh of the water that I shall give him shall never thirst." What a prospect was that for a woman who had drunk deeply from the wells of sin, only to find them wells of vinegar and gall!

It was at this point that the woman offered her first prayer: "Sir, give me this water, that I thirst not."[31] Here we have a confession of need and a recognition that in Jesus the need can be met.

4. *Appeal.*

Things were now at a crisis. It was time to touch the root of the need. Why was she a thirsty soul? Because she was a sinful soul, and only as the sin was dealt with could she know the living water springing up in her heart. "Go, call thy husband," said Jesus,[32] and in that simple command He unveiled the entire life of sin. It is not easy for men and

---

[30]V. 7.
[31]John 4:15.
[32]V. 16.

women to face up to their sin, and this woman sought to hide her shame by introducing a technical difference in religion between the Samaritans and the Jews.[33] At the same time there was no denial of the sin, but rather an admission, when she acclaimed Jesus as a prophet.[34] Even through the shield that she sought to raise against the sharp arrows of conviction, Jesus saw the seeking soul, and did for her what he did for very few, frankly declaring Himself the Messiah for whom she waited.[35] Thus He offered Himself to her for the assuaging of her thirst, for the taking away of her sin, and for the realization of her hope.

5. *Response.*

Her response was complete, and she immediately became an ardent witness for Christ, with the result that Jesus spent two days in the village, where many believed in His name.[36]

This incident is worthy of careful study by those who would deal graciously and wisely with needy souls.

QUESTIONS AND EXERCISES

1. What three spheres of witnessing are presented in the first chapter of John's Gospel?
2. What were the characteristics of the witness given in John 1?
3. Give an analysis of the witness in John 1.
4. Discuss our Lord's techniques in dealing with Nicodemus.
5. Draw a comparison between our Lord's dealing with Nicodemus and His dealing with the Samaritan woman at the well of Sychar.

---

[33]V. 20.
[34]V. 19.
[35]V. 26.
[36]Vv. 39-43.

The Holy Spirit in Soul-Winning

AT VARIOUS STAGES of our study we have stressed the work of the Holy Spirit in soul-winning. He has a work to do in the soul-winner. This includes a work of sanctification to fit the Christian for the task, and the implanting of the divine passion to stir him to the task. Then the Holy Spirit must guide the believer to the soul to whom the witness is to be given, empower and control the witness, and give discernment and wisdom. By the same token, a work of the Holy Spirit must be wrought in the one receiving the witness. There is a preparatory work there, too, of which the one in question may be quite unconscious. The convicting, the enlightening, the converting, the empowering to believe are all part of the Holy Spirit's work, as well as the assuring witness. Without such two-way operation of the Spirit of God, all evangelism, including personal evangelism, is a dead and fruitless affair.

All this is clearly indicated in the Scriptures, as well as realized by those who engage in the sacred task, and all this is illustrated in that great historical treatise on evangelism, the Acts of the Apostles. Here, then, are fourteen propositions concerning the work of the Holy Spirit, as illustrated in the Acts. The student should turn to the Scripture references in the following paragraphs.

A. THE HOLY SPIRIT BESTOWS POWER.[1]

The need for power in the work of evangelism lies in the fact that it engages us in implacable conflict with all the powers of darkness, as well as with the natural enmity of the human heart against God. Now God does not propose to make us strong in ourselves. We are too prone to use what we have in pursuits other than the will of God. The power is vested in the Holy Spirit. "Ye shall receive power, the Holy Spirit coming upon you," is God's answer to our inadequacy, and it is a sufficient answer.

B. THE HOLY SPIRIT GIVES UTTERANCE.[2]

This was one of the first activities of the Spirit when He was given to the one hundred and twenty on the Day of Pentecost. That that utterance was "in other tongues" need not command our attention now. The whole point is that utterance was needed to make the message of the Gospel known to those who were assembled in Jerusalem for the feast from all parts whither the Jews had been dispersed. Moreover, the utterance had to be of such a nature as to convince men that God was at work. The particular form of the utterance, then, belongs to the occasion. Whether the witness is to be given in our own tongue or another, to make it effective the utterance must be given by the Holy Spirit. Being smart will not make us useful in God's service.

C. THE HOLY SPIRIT INSPIRES BOLDNESS.[3]

From two things we need to be delivered—the timidity of the flesh, and the boldness of the flesh. In the work of the Gospel the boldness of the flesh is as detrimental as the timidity of the flesh. Timidity may hinder us from deliver-

[1]Acts 1:8.
[2]Acts 2:4.
[3]Acts 4:29-31.

ing the message, but unholy boldness will drive us to speak
when we ought to be silent, and to speak offensively when
the word ought to be tender and loving. But boldness born
of the Holy Spirit will be the courage of the lion coupled
with the gentleness of the dove.

D. THE HOLY SPIRIT REQUIRES PURITY.[4]

In the story of Ananias and Sapphira we see the jealousy
of the Holy Spirit for the purity of the witness, and His
going about to secure it, even when it meant stern discipline.
He demands that the vessel be clean—"a vessel unto honor,
sanctified, and meet for the master's use."[5] The discipline
required to make us such vessels may at times be severe,
but He will never lower His standards, and surely it is well
worth all that is involved, if only we may bring forth fruit
for the Saviour!

E. THE HOLY SPIRIT CO-OPERATES WITH THE WITNESS.[6]

"We are his witnesses . . . and so is also the Holy Ghost,"
said Peter to the Sanhedrin when challenged by them concerning his right to preach in the name of Jesus. What confidence it gives to know that we are not alone in our witnessing, but that the Holy Spirit is backing up our testimony
concerning the Lord Jesus! If we would have this confidence, we must be led by the Spirit. If we run ahead and
give witness apart from His directing, we shall work alone,
and be utterly lacking in effectiveness. The Holy Spirit is
not at our beck and call, to support what we do on our own
initiative, but if we obey His leading, we shall have His
support. Is not this the secret of many of the frustrating

[4]Acts 5:1-15.
[5]II Tim. 2:21.
[6]Acts 5:32.

experiences of sincere, but willful and independent, personal workers?

F. THE HOLY SPIRIT DIRECTS ORGANIZATION.[7]

This may not seem to bear directly on personal soul-winning, and yet the whole context shows how definitely related was organization to the work of soul-winning. Because of poor organization the spiritual condition of the church suffered, and the spread of the Gospel was slowed down. But when the proper organization was effected, by direction of the Holy Spirit, the spiritual defect was eliminated, and the work of soul-winning leaped ahead. In the case cited in Acts, the organization was needed in the local church. The same Spirit of order will require order in the individual life. Many Christians are lacking in usefulness because of a lack of order. Their lives are cluttered, undisciplined. If they would submit to the direction of the Holy Spirit, they would be whipped into shape, and a regulated life, rid of a thousand unnecessary things, would begin to tell for God. It is a strange heresy that is abroad—that the freedom of the Spirit and lack of organization are synonymous. All God's works reveal Him as a God of order, and the Spirit-directed life will be a life of order.

> Take from our lives the strain and stress,
> And let our *ordered lives* confess
> The beauty of Thy peace.[8]

G. THE HOLY SPIRIT ORDERS EXPANSION.[9]

Expansion is one of the chief items in our Lord's program, and it is a normal expression of a living witness. Where the Holy Spirit is directing, men are seeing farther and farther

[7]Acts 6:1-8.
[8]John Greenleaf Whittier.
[9]Acts 8:1-24.

horizons, and are reaching out, out, out. This characteristic of the Christian movement seems to have been temporarily forgotten by the early church. They were content to consolidate their position in Jerusalem. But the Lord would not allow His people to stop at the starting point, so He stirred up their nest with an intense persecution which scattered the Christians abroad. So the directing Spirit used drastic means to have His program carried out. Read the chapter, and see how the pressure forced the witness throughout Samaria (not only the city but the province), and then for the sequel turn to chapter 11,[10] where we are informed that the same expansion movement spread as far as Phoenicia, Cyprus, and Syrian Antioch. We shall not forget that Antioch became the starting point of another great expansion, associated with the name of Paul. A work directed by the Holy Spirit is an expanding work.

H. THE HOLY SPIRIT BREAKS DOWN BARRIERS.[11]

The Holy Spirit has a way of ignoring the nice distinctions which we human beings so emphasize among ourselves. We have already seen what barriers the Lord Jesus broke through in His dealings with the woman of Samaria.[12] In the Acts of the Apostles we observe the Holy Spirit directing the work of the Gospel along similar lines. Samaritans and Gentiles are called on the same basis as Jews. To us this seems perfectly normal, but it was a revolutionary concept to the Jewish believers of the middle of the first century of this era. Unusual dealings were required to induce Peter to abandon his Jewish prejudices sufficiently to enter a Gentile home and preach the Gospel to a Gentile company. Then it required strong reasoning to persuade

---

[10]Vv. 19-21.
[11]Acts 10:1—11:26
[12]Lesson 14.

the church in Jerusalem that Peter had acted according to the will of God. It was a bold venture for those of the dispersion to preach to Greeks in Antioch, but they were vindicated by the great work of the Spirit in the establishing of a Gentile church there. Most of us have prejudices which erect barriers between us and members of certain groups. The Holy Spirit, if He has control of our lives, will play havoc with our prejudices, and we shall find ourselves overleaping barriers which before seemed so formidable, whether racial, national, social, or religious.

I. The Holy Spirit Overcomes Satanic Power.[13]

We have mentioned the satanic opposition in various aspects of our subject, and do so again to emphasize the fact that the Holy Spirit is God's answer to that opposition. Generally we meet satanic antagonism expressed through men, and it is well for us to remember that men do not constitute our chief foe. They are but agents of the "principalities and powers" against which we contend. We must therefore look to spiritual power to overcome spiritual power, and the Holy Spirit is fully adequate to the task. He is the omnipotent Spirit, against whom the combined forces of Hell cannot stand. Whether the evil powers operate through men, or apart from men, He is able to quell them. Our resource, then, is prayer, with complete confidence that the Holy Spirit will exert His powers against the forces of evil that the will of God may be done.

J. The Holy Spirit Directs the Witness.[14]

The Book of the Acts is full of evidences of such leading, but I have chosen one outstanding example. Paul's desire

---

[13]Acts 13:4-13.
[14]Acts 16:6, 7.

to witness in the province of Asia was rebuked by the Holy Spirit, as was also his urge to carry the Gospel to the wilder region of Bithynia. There was nothing wrong with the apostle's wishes, except that they were not in line with the plan which God had laid out for him and for the spreading of the Gospel, and Paul had to learn that not only the general activity of witnessing for Christ was to be an act of obedience, but also the order of the witnessing. After the two experiences of restraint, he was remarkably led to the next sphere of operation by means of the vision of the man of Macedonia. Effective witnessing is witnessing which is directed by the Holy Spirit, not by natural urges. This may be a difficult lesson to learn. It means curbing the human impulse, and it means recognizing the leading of the Spirit.

K. THE HOLY SPIRIT PREPARES HEARTS.[15]

Very often what seems like an incidental phrase in Scripture is actually the statement of a great principle. So when we read this description of Lydia of Thyatira, the seller of purple in Philippi, "whose heart the Lord opened," we have come upon a great Gospel truth of universal application. No one was ever saved, nor will be saved, of whom it may not be said, "whose heart the Lord opened." How we need to be delivered from the fallacy that our reasoning, our persuasion, our tact are the effective cause of the opening of men's hearts! That is the work of the Holy Spirit. We are indeed bearers of the message, but apart from the Spirit's operation in opening men's hearts, our best reasoning would leave them dark, our sweetest persuasions would find them still obdurate. The revival for which many long will find one of its first expressions in a revival of dependence on the Holy Spirit rather than on methods.

---

[15]Acts 16:14.

L. THE HOLY SPIRIT ENLIGHTENS BELIEVERS.[16]

The apostle Paul considered the enlightening of believers as part of his evangelism. The believers to whom we refer were men who had a disposition to faith, but whose faith was rather of a preliminary sort because of lack of teaching, with the result that they were not experiencing that fullness of life and joy and power which is the portion of the true believer. Such was the case with these disciples at Ephesus, and Paul, discerning the lack, sought to repair it. A work of the Holy Spirit was wrought, and the defective believers were embarked on the full tide of the life of faith. Now we are not likely to meet up with people who are precisely in the same situation as those disciples of Ephesus, "knowing only the baptism of John," but we shall have contact with many defective believers, the victims of imperfect instruction, who give evidence of the lack of sound Gospel teaching in their lives. Instead of criticizing them as "poor examples of Christians" we must take them upon our hearts, and believe that the Holy Spirit will lead them into full understanding as the truth of the Gospel is presented to them.

M. THE HOLY SPIRIT CONFOUNDS MIMICRY.[17]

Even in apostolic days there arose imitations of the work of God. It was evident that the name of Jesus, as invoked by the apostles, was mighty in healing, delivering, and the casting out of demons. Why, then, could not others use that powerful name and so increase their own effectiveness and magnify themselves? This the Jewish exorcists of Ephesus sought to do, but the jealousy of the Holy Spirit against such mimicry was immediately in evidence, so that the

---

[16] Acts 19:1-7.
[17] Acts 19:11-19.

Jewish exorcists were put to confusion. Now, just as the immediate judgment of the Spirit against the hypocrisy of Ananias and Sapphira was not established as the divine method for the whole age, so the immediate judgment of the Spirit upon the Jewish mimics of Ephesus did not become the rule for this age. But the principle remains. The Spirit will judge hypocrisy, and the Spirit will judge mimicry. The processes may be slower, but the end is sure.

> Though the mills of God grind slowly,
> Yet they grind exceeding small;
> Though with patience He stands waiting,
> With exactness grinds He all.[18]

Today we are plagued with imitations; they seem to get results! Nevertheless, we need not be thrown into a panic. The false will end in disaster. Our duty is to pray, especially for those who are caught in the snares of the imitators.

N. THE HOLY SPIRIT GIVES DISCERNMENT.[19]

The passages indicated may seem at first sight to have little reference to personal evangelism, but they are part of a general pattern. Paul, the great soul-winner, discerned the direction in which God was moving, and was able to judge events in the light of that movement. This made him master of the situation, to know what ought to be done. See him in the midst of the Mediterranean storm! Not the centurion, not the shipmaster is the dominant figure, but the preacher! Holy Ghost discernment has made him the man of the hour. We may not all take over direction of a shipwreck in mid-ocean, but we shall all be in situations in

---

[18]Henry Wadsworth Longfellow.
[19]Acts 27:10, 21, 22, 30-34.

which only discernment given us by the Holy Spirit will teach us to do the thing by which men will be saved.

All this leads us to the conclusion that effective soul-winning depends on the control of the Holy Spirit in our lives. "Not by might, nor by power, but by my spirit, saith the Lord of hosts."[20]

QUESTIONS AND EXERCISES

1. The Acts of the Apostles is a great historical treatise on evangelism. Discuss and evaluate this statement.
2. What is the outstanding feature of the work recorded in the Acts? Justify your answer.
3. Why is the power of the Holy Spirit needed in the work of evangelism? Do not confine your answer to the brief statement in this lesson.
4. Show the need for an "ordered" life in the work of the Gospel.
5. Give examples from Acts of the work of the Holy Spirit in guiding, giving utterance, enlightening, disciplining, inspiring boldness.

---

[20]Zech. 4:6.

LESSON 16

Dealing with the Seeker

A. The Anxious.

THIS MAN is convinced of his sinnerhood before God and earnestly desires salvation. Occasionally a person will become so burdened by the weight of his sins and the consciousness of his separation from God that he will seek out the soul-winner to inquire the way of salvation. Or if he does not do the actual seeking, there will be a ready response when he is spoken to on the subject of his salvation; and the personal worker will know immediately that the Holy Spirit has been dealing with him.

1. *Indications of Desire.*

a) He will be anxious to be saved, but he will be ignorant of the way as was Cornelius.[1]

b) He will be anxious to be saved immediately as was the jailer.[2]

c) He will be humble and self-condemned as was the publican.[3]

d) He will be willing to do anything in order to be saved as was Saul of Tarsus.[4]

---

[1]Acts 10:1-48.
[2]Acts 16:30, 31.
[3]Luke 18:13.
[4]Acts 9:6.

e) He may be searching the Scriptures as was the Ethiopian Eunuch.[†]

f) He will listen attentively as did Lydia.[‡]

2. *Methods of Approach.*

a) Show the anxious person Jesus Christ as his Sin-bearer. Often this individual has been seeking to get rid of his sins in his own strength. He has wept and prayed. He has made resolution after resolution, to no avail. He must see that God has laid upon Jesus the iniquity of us all,[5] that Christ bore our sins in His own body on the tree.[6] The Lord Jesus Christ did this all by himself; He did not need our help.[7] Because Christ was made a curse for us, He has redeemed all who believe from the curse of the law.[8] When the person realizes that Christ bore all his sins in His own body when He hung on the cruel cross he very often will accept Christ immediately.

b) The inquirer should be shown from the Word of God that Christ is also the risen Lord. The significance of Christ's resurrection is that the believer has been justified.[9] That means that God the Father looks upon the believer as though he had never sinned, for the record in Heaven against the believer has been removed. God has blotted out as a thick cloud his transgressions, and as a cloud his sins.[10] The person has a new standing before God.

c) Another blessed fact that comes from Christ's resurrection is that Christ is now seated at the right hand of the Father interceding for the believer. He thus is able to save

†Acts 8:26-40.
‡Acts 16:12-15.
⁵Isa. 53:6.
⁶I Pet. 2:24.
⁷Heb. 1:3.
⁸Gal. 3:13.
⁹Rom. 4:25.
¹⁰Isa. 44:22.

unto the uttermost all who draw nigh unto God by Him,[11] and that He is able to guard them from stumbling.[12]

3. *Make Plan of Salvation Simple.*

Explain very carefully to the inquirer how he can make the Lord Jesus Christ his own Saviour and Lord. The Word is very clear and definite on this point. It says: "If thou shalt confess with thy mouth Jesus as Lord, and shalt believe in thy heart that God raised him from the dead, thou shalt be saved."[13] It also says: "But as many as received him, to them gave he power [or authority] to become the sons of God, even to them that believe on his name."[14] Assure the seeker that Jesus Christ is more willing to save than the seeker is to be saved. Jesus said that He is standing and knocking at the heart's door, and that if the person will open the door, He will come in.[15]

4. *Stress Assurance.*

After the person has asked the Lord Jesus to come in, lead him into the assurance of salvation by urging him to believe in the Word of God and not to look to his feelings for this assurance. His feelings will change but God's Word never changes. He is to believe what God has said in His Word. The apostle John wrote: "These things have I written unto you that believe on the name of the Son of God: that ye may know that ye have eternal life, and that ye may believe on the name of the Son of God."[16] Paul also wrote of this assurance: "For I know whom I have believed, and am persuaded that he is able to keep that which I have committed unto him against that day."[17]

---

[11]Heb. 7:25.
[12]Jude 24 (A.S.V.).
[13]Rom. 10:9 (A.S.V.).
[14]John 1:12.
[15]Rev. 3:20.
[16]I John 5:13.
[17]II Tim. 1:12.

B. The Troubled.

This person wants victory over evil habits, or desires help because of serious problems, but feels no need of Christ.

1. *Learn To Detect.*

The personal worker must learn to detect this in the seeker. One must quickly determine whether the individual desires to get to Christ or if he is only seeking victory over a bad habit, for the method of dealing with the person will vary greatly.

One night a young man came forward in a meeting in response to the Gospel invitation. He went into the inquiry room, and I dealt with him. He desired victory over the drink habit and was desperately seeking help. But when I mentioned his need of Christ and the fact that Christ could break this terrible habit and set him free, he immediately informed me that he had no desire for Christ, all he wanted was help to break this habit which had bound him for many years. He would not listen to the Gospel but arising to his feet he left the room.

A young married woman with a very heavy heart came to my study one evening. She was having marital trouble and there was some danger of her being held in contempt of court because she had taken her daughter out of the state after the court had ordered her to remain in the city. Her husband had learned of this fact and was about to inform the court in order to hurt her. She was terrified and talked for four hours of her trouble. When I endeavored to show her that her greatest trouble was not that of her home life, but of sin in her own heart, she could not comprehend such a thing. All she wanted was help for her immediate problems.

2. Method of Dealing.

a) Impress upon this person the fact that God's Word says he is a sinner,[18] and that his sin is against God. Remind him of what David said after his sin had been found out: "Against thee, thee only, have I sinned, and done this evil in thy sight: that thou mightest be justified when thou speakest, and be clear when thou judgest."[19]

b) Sin in the first analysis is rebellion in the heart against a Holy God.

C. The Indifferent to Sin.

This is the seeker after God who is not deeply concerned about the sin question. This person desires to know God, but he does not realize he must approach God through a Mediator, the Lord Jesus Christ.

A friend of mine was once riding in an airplane with a Jewish businessman. The Jewish friend had made some comments about the beauty of the ride and the experience of flying above the clouds. He stated that the person who did not believe in a God was a fool, for there is so much evidence of a divine Creator. He then asked my friend for his views. This man is an ardent Christian and his reply was that he agreed with his business friend, but that he believed God the Father could only be approached through the Lord Jesus Christ. To this statement the Jewish man said:

"Oh, you believe one must approach God through a Mediator."

My friend replied that this was his idea.

"That is not for me," replied the Jew, "I cannot believe in the necessity of a Mediator."

[18]Rom. 3:23.
[19]Ps. 51:4.

1. *Reality of Sin.*

The awfulness of sin must be impressed upon the mind
of the person who desires to know God, but who has little
consciousness of the reality of sin. He must be told, kindly,
but firmly, that there is "none righteous, no, not one,"[20] and
that "all our righteousnesses are as filthy rags"[21] in God's
sight. If the person will believe what the Bible says about
his sinfulness, he will realize the necessity of the Saviour,
the Lord Jesus Christ.

2. *Need for Mediator.*

The individual who cannot believe in the necessity of a
Mediator does not realize that because of his sinfulness he
cannot approach a Holy God. He does not know the truth
that his sins have separated him from God, and that without the shedding of blood there is no possibility of remission
of sin.[22]

3. *Only One Mediator.*

Jesus Christ said there was no approach to God the Father
but through Him.[23] Peter restated this in his epistle when
he wrote: "For Christ also hath once suffered for sins, the
just for the unjust, that he might bring us to God, being put
to death in the flesh, but quickened by the Spirit."[24] Paul
also emphasized this truth.[25]

D. THE UNSATISFIED.

This seeker is longing for peace, satisfaction, and rest.
The group to which this person belongs is very large. The
hearts of many are failing them for fear. Life with its un-

---

[20]Rom. 3:10.
[21]Isa. 64:6.
[22]Heb. 9:22.
[23]John 14:6.
[24]I Peter 3:18.
[25]I Tim. 2:5.

certainties and complexities is too much for many people. They long for peace and rest. They drink of the waters of this world and thirst again. Where can they find satisfaction? To whom can they turn for the solution to their problems and the answers to their questions? They need to turn to the One of whom the psalmist wrote: "For he satisfieth the longing soul, and filleth the hungry soul with goodness."[26]

1. *Christ the Satisfier.*

This person is the Lord Jesus Christ, who said: "Come unto me, all ye that labor and are heavy laden, and I will give you rest. Take my yoke upon you, and learn of me; for I am meek and lowly in heart: and ye shall find rest unto your souls."[27] No other man had ever been able to make such an offer and fulfill it. Other teachers and philosophers have suggested to people how they might find rest, but none has been able to say: "Come to me, and I will give you rest."

2. *Abiding Peace.*

Then there is peace for which people long today: Peace of mind; peace of heart. Many books have been written on the subject of peace and have been eagerly purchased by the multitude. In most of them are suggestions of things which the individual must do in order to rid himself of his fears and thus secure some measure of peace of mind. But the Lord Jesus said: "Peace, I leave with you, my peace I give unto you: not as the world giveth, give I unto you. Let not your heart be troubled, neither let it be afraid."[28]

a) This wonderful peace is His peace. It is not a peace which is the result of human effort in making adjustments with one's surroundings and lot in life. The world has no peace like His peace. It has nothing it can substitute for

---

[26]Ps. 107:9.
[27]Matt. 11:28, 29.
[28]John 14:27.

His peace, and say, "This is just as good." Think of His tranquillity, the inner peace which He experienced all of the time. This is the peace He offers to all who will come to Him.

b) He said again: "These things I have spoken unto you, that in me ye might have peace. In the world ye shall have tribulation: but be of good cheer; I have overcome the world."[29] His peace was not to be that which is the result of having no tribulation, but it is peace in the midst of tribulation. Jesus never promised a life free from tribulation and trial, but He did promise peace of heart and mind when the storms of life were raging, and the black clouds were gathering round.

c) He has given us the reason for such peace.

(1) It is because He has overcome the world and all of its problems and all of its sins. God's peace is the result of knowing that one's sins have been forgiven, and that one is now in contact with the Creator of the universe who is able to meet every need and solve every problem.[30] The apostle Paul wrote: "In nothing be anxious; but in everything by prayer and supplication with thanksgiving let your requests be made known unto God. And the peace of God, which passeth all understanding, shall guard your hearts and your thoughts in Christ Jesus."[31]

(2) Peace is also the result of knowing that the future is sure. The thought of appearing before the Great White Throne to be judged for one's sins is a terrifying thought to many people. But when the truth is known about the hereafter, which God gives in His Word, there comes into the heart a wonderful peace. Paul wrote: "There is there-

---

[29]John 16:33.
[30]Rom. 5:1.
[31]Phil. 4:6, 7 (A.S.V.).

fore now no condemnation to them which are in Christ
Jesus. . . . For the law of the Spirit of life in Christ Jesus
hath made me free from the law of sin and death."[32]

QUESTIONS AND EXERCISES

1. Give some evidences that will be recognized in the seeker
   who is anxious to be saved.
2. Why should Christ be presented to the seeker as the Sin-
   bearer and risen Lord?
3. To what is the seeker to look for assurance of salvation?
4. Discuss the method of dealing with a seeker who wants victory over evil habits, but who feels no need of Christ.
5. What verses of Scripture can be used with the person who
   desires to know God, but who is not concerned with the
   problem of sin?
6. Give five verses of Scripture which can be used with the
   seeker who is desiring rest and peace.

---

[32]Rom. 8:1, 2.

LESSON 17

Dealing with the Self-righteous

THE SELF-RIGHTEOUS PERSON is sometimes very difficult to reach because he is so satisfied with himself. He thinks God must be greatly impressed with him, and must have the same opinion of him that he has of himself.

A. GOD'S VIEW OF THE SELF-RIGHTEOUS.

This person must be brought to realize that the Bible says there is none righteous, no not one;[1] and that all of our righteousnesses are as filthy rags in God's sight.[2] These verses give God's opinion of the individual. The self-righteous person needs to see himself as God sees him. God said of the nation of Israel that the whole head was sick and the whole heart was faint; that from the sole of the foot unto the head there was no soundness in it, but wounds and bruises and putrefying sores.[3] This was not merely true of a nation years ago, but it is a very true picture of every self-righteous person today.

The Lord Jesus Christ spoke very emphatically against the self-righteous people of His day. They were the Pharisees who prided themselves in their religious acts and good character. They gave liberally of their money. It has been estimated that with their tithes, offerings, and alms they

---

[1]Rom. 3:10.
[2]Isa. 64:6.
[3]Isa. 1:6.

162

gave 27 per cent of their income. They read the Old Testament every day, and endeavored to observe all the stated feasts and ceremonies. They prayed at least three times each day. They were moral and cultured and bragged about it. Yet the Lord Jesus Christ spoke scathing words against them. He said: "For I say unto you, That except your righteousness shall exceed the righteousness of the scribes and Pharisees, ye shall in no case enter into the kingdom of heaven."[4]

"And he spake this parable unto certain which trusted in themselves that they were righteous, and despised others: Two men went up into the temple to pray; the one a Pharisee, and the other a publican. The Pharisee stood and prayed thus within himself, God, I thank thee, that I am not as other men are, extortioners, unjust, adulterers, or even as this publican. I fast twice in the week, I give tithes of all that I possess. And the publican, standing afar off, would not lift up so much as his eyes unto heaven, but smote upon his breast, saying, God be merciful to me a sinner. I tell you, this man went down to his house justified rather than the other: for everyone that exalteth himself shall be abased; and he that humbleth himself shall be exalted."[5]

B. NECESSITY OF NEW BIRTH.

Jesus said to the Pharisee Nicodemus, who was one of the best men who ever lived in the city of Jerusalem: "Verily, verily, I say unto thee, Except a man be born again, he cannot see the kingdom of God. . . . Verily, verily, I say unto thee, Except a man be born of water and of the Spirit, he cannot enter into the kingdom of God. That which is born of the flesh is flesh; and that which is born of the Spirit

---

[4]Matt. 5:20.
[5]Luke 18:9-14.

is spirit. Marvel not that I said unto thee, Ye must be born again."[6]

The apostle Paul was a self-righteous Pharisee before his conversion,[7] but after he had been a Christian for many years, he wrote: "Yea doubtless, and I count all things but loss for the excellency of the knowledge of Christ Jesus my Lord: for whom I have suffered the loss of all things, and do count them but dung, that I may win Christ, and be found in him, not having mine own righteousness, which is of the law, but that which is through the faith of Christ, the righteousness which is of God by faith."[8]

C. INSUFFICIENCY OF GOOD WORKS.

The self-righteous must be told that salvation is not based on an individual's good works. This is clearly taught in the Scriptures: "For by grace are ye saved through faith; and that not of yourselves: it is the gift of God: not of works, lest any man should boast."[9] "Not by works of righteousness which we have done, but according to his mercy he saved us, by the washing of regeneration, and renewing of the Holy Ghost; which he shed on us abundantly through Jesus Christ our Saviour; that being justified by his grace, we should be made heirs according to the hope of eternal life."[10]

D. SUFFICIENCY OF CHRIST'S RIGHTEOUSNESS.

That self-righteousness will not suffice is proved by the fact that a person must have the righteousness of Christ in order to be saved. It is not our righteousness that makes us fit for Heaven, but Christ's righteousness. The Scrip-

---

[6]John 3:3, 5-7.
[7]Acts 9:1-20.
[8]Phil. 3:8, 9.
[9]Eph. 2:8, 9.
[10]Titus 3:5-7.

ture states that all our righteousnesses are as filthy rags.[11] That being true, the only righteousness of value is the imputed righteousness of Jesus Christ.[12]

E. GOD'S PROVISION IN GRACE.

If one could gain Heaven by his good works and fine character, it would be a reward earned, but salvation is a gift given to the one who believes on the Lord Jesus Christ, and comes from God's grace. Paul wrote: "For the grace of God that bringeth salvation hath appeared to all men."[13]

Grace is God doing for us that which we do not deserve. No one deserves salvation, but God has provided it as a gift because of His marvelous grace. God has no salvation for the self-righteous person, for Christ said that He did not come to call the righteous, but sinners to repentance.[14] He came seeking lost people.[15]

Salvation has been provided by God for the one who believes on Jesus Christ, because the work that Christ did at Calvary when He shed His blood, enables God the Father to forgive the sins of the believer.[16] It therefore stands to reason that the individual who will not trust Christ cannot receive the efficacy of the shed blood of Christ.

The self-righteous person does not have the Holy Spirit living in him because he has never received Christ into his heart. Therefore he does not belong to Christ. The Bible says: "Now if any man have not the Spirit of Christ, he is none of his."[17]

---

[11]Isa. 64:6.
[12]Phil. 3:3-7; Rom. 3:21-26.
[13]Titus 2:11.
[14]Luke 5:32.
[15]Luke 19:10.
[16]Eph. 1:7.
[17]Rom. 8:9.

F. AWARENESS OF SINS.

The Christian worker should show the self-righteous person that everyone who has come into the presence of God has instantly become conscious of his sins and his sinful condition. There are some great illustrations of this in the Bible.

Job said: "I have heard of thee by the hearing of the ear: but now mine eye seeth thee. Wherefore I abhor myself, and repent in dust and ashes."[18]

Isaiah the prophet saw the Lord high and lifted up, and he cried: "Woe is me! for I am undone; because I am a man of unclean lips, and I dwell in the midst of a people of unclean lips: for mine eyes have seen the King, the Lord of hosts."[19]

The apostle Paul before his conversion was a self-righteous Pharisee, but many years after the Lord Jesus had saved him[20] he wrote: "Though I might also have confidence in the flesh. If any other man thinketh that he hath whereof he might trust in the flesh, I more: circumcised the eighth day, of the stock of Israel, of the tribe of Benjamin, an Hebrew of the Hebrews; as touching the law, a Pharisee; concerning zeal, persecuting the church; touching the righteousness which is in the law, blameless. But what things were gain to me, those I counted loss for Christ. Yea doubtless, and I count all things but loss for the excellency of the knowledge of Christ Jesus my Lord: for whom I have suffered the loss of all things, and do count them but dung, that I may win Christ, and be found in him, not having mine own righteousness, which is of the law, but that which

---

[18]Job 42:5, 6.
[19]Isa. 6:5.
[20]Acts 9:1-20.

is through the faith of Christ, the righteousness which is of God by faith."[21]

G. THE ONLY WAY TO GOD.

The only robe of righteousness which makes a person fit for God's presence and the court of Heaven is that one which is a gift from God received by faith in the Lord Jesus Christ."[22]

QUESTIONS AND EXERCISES

1. Define the word self-righteousness.
2. Give two Bible verses which reveal God's thought about self-righteousness.
3. Why did Jesus speak so emphatically to Nicodemus on the necessity of the new birth?
4. Prove from Scripture that salvation is not based on an individual's good works.
5. Who were the people Jesus was able to help when He was on earth?
6. Give illustrations from Scripture of those who have become convicted of their sinfulness when they came into God's presence.
7. What robe of righteousness does God approve?

---

[21]Phil. 3:4-9.
[22]Isa. 61:10; Phil. 3:8, 9.

LESSON 18

Dealing with the Procrastinator

THIS PERSON does not deny the necessity of salvation, nor its importance. He hopes to be saved some day before he dies, but not today. Secretly he desires to enjoy the pleasures of sin for a season. He wants to "sow some wild oats," and "have some fun," before he turns to Christ.

A. LED BY SATAN.

The procrastinator does not realize he is being led on by Satan who constantly seeks to keep people from coming to Christ. The Bible speaks of salvation in the present tense. Never is it referred to as something one will eventually need; rather it is described as a present necessity. The little word *now* is a very important word in God's vocabulary of salvation.

"Come now, and let us reason together, saith the Lord: though your sins be as scarlet, they shall be as white as snow; though they be red like crimson, they shall be as wool."[1] "Now is the accepted time; behold, now is the day of salvation."[2]

God urges the individual to be saved *now;* tomorrow may be too "late." It is never an optional matter.

If Satan can keep the person procrastinating, he will keep that one unsaved. He is the originator of the thought,

---

[1] Isa. 1:18.
[2] II Cor. 6:2.

"Not now, maybe tomorrow"; and tomorrow never comes for many.

B. Result of Procrastination.

For one to die without Christ means eternal separation from God. It includes all that Christ meant when He used such words as *perish;*[3] *lost;*[4] *destruction.*[5] Life is so uncertain, it behooves everyone to prepare for the hereafter. James wrote: "Whereas ye know not what shall be on the morrow. For what is your life? It is even a vapor, that appeareth for a little time, and then vanisheth away."[6] A person's life is also likened to the grass which in the morning groweth up, and at noontime is cut down and withered.[7]

The procrastinator should also remember that "whatsoever a man soweth, that shall he also reap";[8] and that "he that soweth to his flesh shall of the flesh reap corruption."[9] No one can sow "wild oats" without reaping a harvest.

C. Some Excuses.

Here are some of the most common excuses people give to delay their coming to Christ,[10] followed by pertinent Scriptures to be used in each case.

1. *"Not today."*

"For yourselves know perfectly that the day of the Lord so cometh as a thief in the night. For when they shall say, Peace and safety; then sudden destruction cometh upon

---

[3]John 3:16.
[4]Luke 19:10.
[5]Matt. 7:13.
[6]James 4:14.
[7]Ps. 90:5, 6.
[8]Gal. 6:7.
[9]Gal. 6:8.
[10]Suggested by J. C. Macaulay.

them, as travail upon a woman with child; and they shall not escape."[11]

"Seek ye the Lord while he may be found, call ye upon him while he is near: let the wicked forsake his way, and the unrighteous man his thoughts: and let him return unto the Lord, and he will have mercy upon him; and to our God, for he will abundantly pardon."[12]

"Boast not thyself of tomorrow; for thou knowest not what a day may bring forth."[13]

2. "Wait until I am older."

"Remember now thy Creator in the days of thy youth, while the evil days come not, nor the years draw nigh, when thou shalt say, I have no pleasure in them."[14]

"But exhort one another daily, while it is called Today; lest any of you be hardened through the deceitfulness of sin."[15]

3. "Wait until I am established in business."

"Take heed, and beware of covetousness: for a man's life consisteth not in the abundance of the things which he possesseth." (Read very carefully the parable that Jesus spoke following this injunction.)[16]

"But seek ye first the kingdom of God, and his righteousness; and all these things shall be added unto you."[17]

4. "Wait until I feel moved."

What kind of a feeling should one have before he will flee from grave danger? If the building in which this person resides were to catch fire, would he be so silly as to say he needed a certain emotional feeling before he made his way

---

[11] I Thess. 5:2, 3.
[12] Isa. 55:6, 7.
[13] Prov. 27:1.
[14] Eccles. 12:1.
[15] Heb. 3:13.
[16] Luke 12:15-21.
[17] Matt. 6:33.

to safety, or would he be justified in fleeing simply because he had been warned of impending danger? The answer is too obvious for comment.

God has commanded all men everywhere to repent, the reason being "because he hath appointed a day, in the which he will judge the world in righteousness by that man whom he hath ordained; whereof he hath given assurance unto all men, in that he hath raised him from the dead."[18] A soldier in the service when commanded to do something does not dare say to the commanding officer, "I will if I feel moved." The God of the universe has commanded men to repent, or come to judgment. One's feelings are not to be consulted.

5. *"Wait until I improve myself."*

But Jesus never said to Matthew the publican, "Improve yourself and then come to me."[19] He never refused to see Zaccheus because he had not "improved himself."[20] He shouted to him: "Zaccheus, make haste, and come down; for today I must abide at thy house."

On one occasion he told of two men going into the temple to pray. One was a Pharisee who bragged to God about how good a man he was. He compared himself with the publican and told God that he was not guilty of many of the sins which the publican had committed. The publican beat upon his breast saying, "God be merciful to me a sinner." Jesus said: "I tell you, this man went down to his house justified rather than the other: for everyone that exalteth himself shall be abased; and he that humbleth himself shall be exalted."[21]

6. *"It Costs Too Much."*

The person who says this feels that becoming a Chris-

---

[18]Acts 17:30, 31.
[19]Luke 5:27-32.
[20]Luke 19:1-10.
[21]Luke 18:9-14.

tian will be too costly. That is, he feels he will have to give up too much of the world's pleasures and interests, or he may have to give up his business or position which is definitely not Christian. Show him that the cost of coming to Christ is as nothing compared with the cost of *not* coming to Christ.

Dr. R. A. Torrey used to preach a sermon entitled, "What It Costs Not To Be a Christian."[22] His points were as follows:

a) Not to be a Christian costs the sacrifice of peace, peace of conscience and peace of heart.

b) Not to be a Christian costs the sacrifice of joy, of the highest, purest, truest, most satisfying, and most enduring joy that is to be found here on earth.

c) Not to be a Christian costs the sacrifice of hope of eternal life.

d) Not to be a Christian costs the sacrifice of the highest manhood and womanhood.

e) Not to be a Christian costs the sacrifice of God's favor.

f) Not to be a Christian costs the sacrifice of Christ's acknowledgment in the world to come.

g) Not to be a Christian costs the sacrifice of eternal life, and means to perish forever.

"For what shall it profit a man, if he shall gain the whole world, and lose his own soul?"[23]

QUESTIONS AND EXERCISES

1. Give some Scripture verses which teach that salvation is a present necessity.
2. Why should a person not put off the obtaining of salvation?
3. List the excuses the procrastinator gives for not coming to Christ. Answer these excuses.

---

[22]R. A. Torrey, *Soul-Winning Sermons* (Westwood, N. J.: Revell).
[23]Mark 8:36.

Dealing with Those Who Have Fears

A. THE PERSON WHO IS AFRAID HE IS TOO GREAT A SINNER.

THE PERSONAL WORKER will occasionally encounter an individual who will make this claim. He feels he is beyond salvation, that God will not have anything to do with him, for his sins are too many and too heinous.

1. *Wrong Impression.*

Of course this person is under the impression God is only interested in good people, that is, those who have not committed many of the sins he has. His catalog may include immorality, theft, hatred, and even murder.

2. *Method in Handling.*

This individual should be brought to realize that God loves all sinners, and that he is included in the "whosoever" of John 3:16.

a) Have him read the following verses, and ask him if he is not to be found in one of the four groups herein mentioned: "For when we were yet *without strength,* in due time Christ died for the *ungodly.* For scarcely for a righteous man will one die: yet peradventure for a good man some would even dare to die. But God commendeth his love toward us, in that, while we were yet *sinners,* Christ died for us. Much more then, being now justified by his blood, we shall be saved from wrath through him. For if, when we were *enemies,* we were reconciled to God by the death of his Son, much more, being reconciled, we shall be saved by his life."[1]

b) Show him the Scripture that God is not willing that any should perish, but that all should come to repentance;[2] and that God would have all men to be saved and to come to a knowledge of the truth.[3]

c) Impress upon his mind that the blood of Christ is sufficient to cleanse from all sin. Peter wrote this in his first epistle: "Forasmuch as ye know that ye were not redeemed with corruptible things, as silver and gold, from your vain conversation received by tradition from your fathers; but with the precious blood of Christ, as of a lamb without blemish and without spot."[4]

d) Call to his attention some of the desperate sinners mentioned in the Bible whom God cleansed, forgave, and saved. There was David, who was guilty of adultery and murder.[5] There was Mary Magdalene, out of whom Jesus cast seven demons.[6] Then there was the sinful woman who came and washed Christ's feet with her tears, and to whom He said so tenderly, "Thy sins are forgiven. . . . Thy faith hath saved thee; go in peace."[7]

e) Many of the members of the Corinthian church had been saved out of great sin. Paul reminded them of this when he wrote: "Know ye not that the unrighteous shall not inherit the kingdom of God? Be not deceived: neither fornicators, nor idolaters, nor adulterers, nor effeminate, nor abusers of themselves with mankind, nor thieves, nor covetous, nor drunkards, nor revilers, nor extortioners, shall in-

---

[1] Rom. 5:6-10.
[2] II Peter 3:9.
[3] I Tim. 2:4.
[4] I Peter 1:18, 19.
[5] Ps. 32 and Ps. 51.
[6] Mark 16:9.
[7] Luke 7:37-50.

herit the kingdom of God. And such were some of you: but ye are washed, but ye are sanctified, but ye are justified in the name of the Lord Jesus, and by the Spirit of our God."[8]

f) Perhaps this troubled soul will claim that he has resisted God's invitation to come again and again, and that he fears God will not have anything more to do with him. Warn him of the danger of the unsaved state, for should he die in this condition, he would be eternally lost. Urge him, therefore, to come immediately to Christ who said, "Him that cometh to me I will in no wise cast out."[9] Assure him that the least yearning he may have in his heart for God was placed there by the Holy Spirit, who is seeking to woo him to Christ.

B. THE PERSON WHO IS AFRAID HE CANNOT HOLD OUT.

This group of people are sad of heart. They realize there is such a blessing as salvation, and they desire it.

1. *Attitude.*

They look with a pathetic wistfulness at happy Christians who are enjoying God's salvation, and wish they could experience it too. But, they say, they have tried over and over again to remain good, and they have always failed. Therefore they have concluded they are not strong enough in themselves to overcome temptation and evil habits. They do not have the moral stamina to hold out against the desires of the flesh.

2. *How To Deal with the Weak and Fearful.*

a) In dealing with such a person, make sure first of all that the individual has definitely received the Lord Jesus Christ for himself. The promise is: "But as many as received him, to them he gave power to become the sons

---

[8] I Cor. 6:9-11.
[9] John 6:37.

of God, even to them that believe on his name."[10] Often
the person who has this fear of not being able to hold out
has been believing *about* Christ; he has never had a definite
meeting with the Saviour.

Some years ago I was chaplain of the Berry Schools in
Mount Berry, Georgia. At the close of one of the Wednesday
evening faculty prayer meetings, a young woman who was
the associate professor of Physics, came to me and said: "I
have always believed about Christ, but I do not think I am
saved."

After talking with her for a few minutes I realized she
had never received the Lord Jesus Christ for herself. So I
explained the way of salvation as simply as I could.

Two weeks later I spoke to the college and high school
students on the subject, "How To Know You Are Saved."
At the conclusion of the service I gave an invitation, asking
those who wanted this assurance to indicate it by raising the
hand. Many responded, but the hand of this young teacher
was not raised.

After the service was concluded, as was my custom, I
stood in front of the college church to greet the students as
they marched out to their dormitories to prepare for the
noon meal. After they had marched out, the faculty and
staff came out. This young woman was among the first of
the faculty to leave the building. She gripped my hand and
said: "I beat you by two weeks."

I knew what she meant. She had gone to her room that
night after the faculty prayer meeting and had asked the
Lord Jesus to come into her heart. He did, and she knew it.

So make sure the friend with whom you are dealing has
definitely received Christ into his heart, for the approach
will then be clear to you.

---

[10]John 1:12.

b) Impress upon the heart that holding out depends on God, and not upon the individual. Jesus spoke with authority when He said: "My sheep hear my voice, and I know them, and they follow me: and I give unto them eternal life; and they shall never perish, neither shall any *man* pluck them out of my hand. My Father, which gave them me, is greater than all; and no *man* is able to pluck them out of my Father's hand. I and my Father are one."[11]

c) Another reason why God is able to keep all who come to Him through Jesus Christ is that Christ is an ever-living Intercessor, who is daily praying for them. In the Epistle to the Hebrews are these assuring words: "Wherefore he is able also to save them to the uttermost that come unto God by him, seeing he ever liveth to make intercession for them."[12]

The Epistle to the Romans contains this same truth: "But God commendeth his love toward us, in that, while we were yet sinners, Christ died for us. Much more then, being now justified by his blood, we shall be saved from wrath through him. For if, when we were enemies, we were reconciled to God by the death of his Son, much more being reconciled, we shall be saved by his life."[13] The idea is, "we shall be kept saved by his life." The believer is kept saved by the life the Lord Jesus Christ is living now at the right hand of the Father. This truth does away with the fear some have of not being able to keep themselves saved.

3. *How To Deal with the Skeptical.*

However, some skeptical soul may say, "It is all very well for you to quote these verses about God's being able to keep, but how do I know He is willing to keep me?"

a) Take this one back over the verses just quoted, laying

---

[11]John 10:27-30.
[12]Heb. 7:25.
[13]Rom. 5:8-10.

emphasis on the words, "that come unto God by him." Point out the fact that God has reconciled enemies to Himself through Jesus Christ. If He has gone to such length to save us when we were His enemies, will He not keep His own who are now His children through Christ? Nowhere does He even intimate we are on our own, or that there are some whom He will not keep. Remember, when we are saved, we are described as being in Christ. It is not an optional matter with God whether or not He will keep those related to His Son.

b) Still another assuring reason that holding out depends upon God and not upon the individual, is to be found in the fact that the Holy Spirit, who has come to indwell the believer, will never leave him. The Lord Jesus spoke this truth to His disciples: "If ye love me, keep my commandments. And I will pray the Father, and he shall give you another Comforter, that he may abide with you forever; even the Spirit of truth; whom the world cannot receive, because it seeth him not, neither knoweth him: but ye know him; for he dwelleth with you, and shall be in you."[14]

The Holy Spirit is thus responsible for getting the believers home to glory. This is what Paul meant when he wrote: "And grieve not the Holy Spirit of God, whereby ye are sealed unto the day of redemption."[15]

c) Another helpful approach is to remind this fearful soul of Paul's argument to the Corinthian Christians. He used the human body and the relationship of the members of the body to the head, as an illustration of the believer's relationship to Christ. "For as the body is one, and hath many members, and all the members of that one body, being many, are one body: so also is Christ. For by one Spirit are

---

[14]John 14:15-17.
[15]Eph. 4:30.

we all baptized into one body, whether we be Jews or Gentiles, whether we be bond or free; and have been all made to drink into one Spirit. For the body is not one member, but many. . . . Now ye are the body of Christ, and members in particular."[16] The fingers of the hand do not need to hold onto the hand, nor does the hand hold onto the arm, and likewise the arm onto the body. The members of the body are part of the body and receive their life from the body. The body is not an organization but an organism.

C. THE PERSON WHO IS AFRAID HE IS NOT ONE OF THE ELECT.

The subject of election, predestination, foreordination is not discussed today as it was some years ago. Many today have no idea of the meaning of these words.

1. *Meaning of Term.*

Occasionally one will meet an individual who has the fear he is not one of the elect, being under the impression he has not been chosen to salvation by God.

2. *Scriptures To Use.*

God has only one message for the unsaved person. It is embodied in the word *whosoever,* and other words of kindred meaning. It is found in such passages as the following:

"For God so loved the world, that he gave his only begotten Son, that whosoever believeth in him should not perish, but have everlasting life."[17]

"The Lord is not slack concerning his promise, as some men count slackness; but is long-suffering to usward, not willing that any should perish, but that all should come to repentance."[18]

The Lord Jesus Christ also said: "And him that cometh

---

[16] I Cor. 12:12-14, 27.
[17] John 3:16.
[18] II Peter 3:9.

to me I will in no wise cast out."[19] Ask the friend who is
fearful to put the Lord Jesus to the test. Let him approach
Christ in earnest belief, and he will find that Christ will
receive him.

D. The Person Who Is Afraid He Has Committed the Unpardonable Sin.

This fear will often throw the person into a feeling of
hopelessness that is alarming. I have known of individuals
who have developed a definite psychosis because of thinking they had committed this sin.

1. *Some Things Not to Do.*

There are some very definite things to guard against when
dealing with such a person.

a) Do not take it for granted that this awful sin has been
committed simply because the individual says so.

b) Never tell anyone he has committed this sin. Your
diagnosis may be wrong, and you would only plunge him
into deeper despair.

c) On the other hand, do not tell the individual he has
not committed this sin, for his confidence would then rest
in your word and not in the Word of God.

2. *Some Things to Do.*

a) Ask him if he hates Christ with an all-consuming hatred.
He will undoubtedly reply that he does not hate Christ, but
that he is anxious to get to Him. Inform him then that the
persons to whom Jesus referred when He spoke about this
sin hated Him and desired to put Him to death. They
wanted nothing to do with Him. So the mere fact that he
does not have this terrible attitude puts him immediately into a different class.

b) Endeavor to find out why he thinks he has committed

---

[19]John 6:37.

this sin. He may give one or more of several reasons.

(1) He may say he has blasphemed God, and has often taken the name of God and of Christ in blasphemy. Do not minimize the fact that this is an awful thing to do, but point out the fact that Jesus said: "Wherefore I say unto you, All manner of sin and blasphemy shall be forgiven unto men. . . . And whosoever speaketh a word against the Son of man, it shall be forgiven him."[20]

Point out to him that the man who became the greatest apostle and Christian leader said that before he was saved he was a blasphemer.[21]

(2) He may say he has been a reviler and a persecutor of Christ. Tell him about the thief on the cross who reviled Christ, but later confessed Christ and heard Him say: "Today shalt thou be with me in paradise."[22]

Many in the multitude who reviled Christ when He hung upon the cross[23] were in the crowd on the Day of Pentecost and heard Peter say: "Therefore let all the house of Israel know assuredly, that God hath made that same Jesus, whom ye have crucified, both Lord and Christ." They cried out, having been convicted in their hearts: "Men and brethren, what shall we do?" To this Peter replied: "Repent, and be baptized every one of you in the name of Jesus Christ for the remission of sins, and ye shall receive the gift of the Holy Ghost. For the promise is unto you, and to your children, and to all that are afar off, even as many as the Lord our God shall call."[24] The result was that about three thousand confessed Christ. So assure the fearful one that reviling Christ is not the unpardonable sin.

---

[20]Matt. 12:31, 32.
[21]I Tim. 1:12, 13.
[22]Luke 23:39-43.
[23]Matt. 27:39.
[24]Acts 2:36-39.

(3) He may say he has lied to God. Turn to Mark 14:66-72, and read to him the experience of Peter. When he denied his Lord, he claimed that he never knew Christ. Jesus did not cast him off, for immediately after Christ's resurrection the angel in the tomb said to the women: "Go your way, tell his disciples and Peter that he goeth before you into Galilee: there ye shall see him, as he said unto you."[25]

(4) The person may claim to be a drunkard and unchaste. Assure him of the fact that Christ Jesus came to save sinners;[26] that He said He had come to seek and to save the lost.[27] Nowhere and at no time did Jesus say that He had come only to save a certain class of sinners. Point out the fact that the church at Corinth had in its membership people who had committed all forms of sin. Paul wrote: "Know ye not that the unrighteous shall not inherit the kingdom of God? Be not deceived: neither fornicators, nor idolaters, nor adulterers, nor effeminate, nor abusers of themselves with mankind, nor thieves nor covetous, nor drunkards, nor revilers, nor extortioners, shall inherit the kingdom of God. And such were some of you; but ye are washed, but ye are sanctified, but ye are justified in the name of the Lord Jesus, and by the Spirit of our God."[28]

(5) Our friend may claim he has committed murder and therefore can have no forgiveness. Remind him of David's experience of adultery with Bath-sheba, and then of his purposely planning the death of her husband in order to cover up his sin of unchastity.[29] God sent the prophet Nathan to David who reminded him of the fact that God knew about his sin. The Fifty-first and the Thirty-second Psalms

---

[25]Mark 16:7.
[26]I Tim. 1:15.
[27]Luke 19:10.
[28]I Cor. 6:9-11.
[29]II Sam. 11.

are the record of David's confession, and of his forgiveness and restoration.

Impress upon this troubled one, Isaiah 1:18: "Come now, and let us reason together, saith the Lord: though your sins be as scarlet, they shall be as white as snow; though they be red like crimson, they shall be as wool."

(6) The person may say that he has rejected Christ again and again, and he feels he has sinned away his day of grace. This is a dangerous thing to do, and can prove fatal, but it is not to be confounded with the unpardonable sin. If there is still a yearning in the heart, be it ever so faint, it is an indication that the Holy Spirit is still wooing. Remind our friend of the words of Christ: "Him that cometh to me I will in no wise cast out."[30] Tell him to prove Christ by coming to Him. The question is not that of Christ's reluctance to accept him, but of his unwillingness to come. Jesus meant that when He said: "Ye will not come to me, that ye might have life."[31] It is a matter of the individual's will.

(7) Occasionally one will find a person who says he has no desire to become a Christian and who thinks that this is the unpardonable sin. It may be well to inquire into the cause, for this may be due to mere indifference rather than to a willful and deliberate act of blasphemy against the Holy Ghost. Show this one that he is a sinner,[32] and that the wages of sin is death,[33] which is eternal separation from the living God. This is called the second death[34] and means an eternity in the lake of fire in company with the Devil and his angels. Try to jar the indifferent one with these sledge-

---

[30] John 6:37.
[31] John 5:40.
[32] Rom. 3:23.
[33] Rom. 6:23.
[34] Rev. 20:11-15.

hammer blows from the Word of God. Trust the Holy
Spirit to apply the Word as you give it out.

3. *Make Meaning of Term Clear.*

Explain from the Scriptures what the unpardonable sin
really is, for there is much misunderstanding concerning it.
If one listens to many evangelists, he gets the impression
that there are unpardonable sins rather than one unpardonable sin. This is due to the fact that men speak of many
different things as constituting this sin.

The Scriptures which are the basis for the term *unpardonable sin*, are Matthew 12:22-32; Mark 3:22-30; Luke 12:10.
You will note that the words *unpardonable sin* are not used,
but that Jesus spoke of blasphemy against the Holy Ghost
as that sin which shall not be forgiven, neither in this
world, neither in the world to come.

One must understand the context, or that which led up
to these words of Christ. Jesus had just healed a demon-
possessed person. The explanation of the Pharisees was that
He had healed this person in the strength of Beelzebub, the
prince of the demons. But Jesus claimed He had done this
in the power of the Holy Spirit, and that their claim was
blasphemy against the Holy Spirit. I feel Mark makes a very
significant statement when in his Gospel account he wrote
by inspiration: "Because they said, He hath an unclean
spirit."[35] They asserted that Jesus Christ was demon-possessed, that He was filled with an unclean spirit, when all
the time He was filled with the Holy Spirit.

As I understand this subject, the unpardonable sin is not
the mere rejection of Jesus Christ as Saviour and Lord
(which is a very serious thing), but it is deliberately saying
that Jesus Christ was demon-possessed while He was on
this earth, and that He performed His miracles in the spirit

---

[35]Mark 3:30.

of the Devil, when He was Spirit-filled and did all of His work in the power of the Holy Spirit.

E. THE PERSON WHO IS AFRAID OF PERSECUTION.

The Scriptures plainly teach that persecution is part of the walk of the Christian.

Paul wrote: "Yea, and all that will live godly in Christ Jesus shall suffer persecution."[36]

Jesus said: "The disciple is not above his master, nor the servant above his lord. It is enough for the disciple that he be as his master, and the servant as his lord. If they have called the master of the house Beelzebub, how much more shall they call them of his household?"[37]

Christ also said: "Blessed are they that are persecuted for righteousness' sake: for theirs is the kingdom of heaven. Blessed are ye, when men shall revile you, and persecute you, and shall say all manner of evil against you falsely, for my sake. Rejoice, and be exceeding glad: for great is your reward in heaven: for so persecuted they the prophets which were before you."[38]

The Christian is in the Devil's territory. He has been saved out of the world and hence is not of the world; but he has not been taken out of the world so far as his bodily presence is concerned, for Jesus said He has sent him into the world. This world hated Christ and it will hate His followers.[39] So the Christian is to arm himself with the mind of Christ as Peter wrote: "Forasmuch then as Christ hath suffered for us in the flesh, arm yourselves likewise with the same mind: for he that hath suffered in the flesh hath ceased from sin."[40]

---

[36]II Tim. 3:12.
[37]Matt. 10:24-28.
[38]Matt. 5:10-12.
[39]John 17:14-18.
[40]I Peter 4:1.

QUESTIONS AND EXERCISES

1. Give the verses of Scripture which should be used with the individual who fears he is too great a sinner.
2. Name some of the great sinners in the Bible whom God called to Himself.
3. What is the first thing to determine when dealing with one who is afraid he can't hold out?
4. Give Scripture verses to prove that "holding out" is God's responsibility.
5. What is God's message for one who is afraid he is not one of the elect?
6. What opinions should be guarded against when dealing with one who thinks he has committed the unpardonable sin?
7. List some of the reasons people give for thinking they have committed this sin.
8. Explain the meaning of the term, *unpardonable sin.*
9. Give Scripture to prove that persecution is often part of the Christian experience

LESSON 20

Miscellaneous Objections

A. "I CANNOT GIVE UP MY SIN."

1. Ask Him Whether He Wants to Be Free from Sin.

ASK THE PERSON who has given this as a reason why he cannot come to Christ, if he really wants to be free from his sinful habits. Jesus said: "Men loved darkness rather than light because their deeds were evil."[1] He also said: "And ye will not come to me, that ye might have life."[2] Determine if the individual is desirous of living in his sin, or if he is in earnest about desiring to come to Christ but is under the impression he must free himself of sinful habits, which thing he knows he cannot do.

2. Show Him Christ Is Only Answer.

Agree with the fact that he cannot give up his sin, for the Lord Jesus Christ said: "Verily, verily, I say unto you, Whosoever committeth sin is the servant [slave] of sin."[3] A slave in Jesus' day was never capable of setting himself free, he had to be freed by someone else. So Jesus continued: "If the Son therefore shall make you free, ye shall be free indeed."[4] He is very able to set the prisoner free, and He loves to do it.

3. Point Him to Christ.

If the person is sincerely seeking, point him to Christ who

[1] John 3:19.
[2] John 5:40.
[3] John 8:34.
[4] John 8:36.

187

said He is able to set a person free. Remind him that Christ is now seated at the right hand of the Father, and that He is able to save to the uttermost all that draw nigh unto God by Him, because He ever liveth to make intercession for them.[5]

4. *Assure Him of New Life.*

Another fact to give this one is that when one believes on the Lord Jesus Christ he becomes a new person, for the Bible says: "Therefore if any man be in Christ, he is a new creature: old things are passed away; behold, all things are become new."[6] He receives a new life, he has a new destiny, a new spirit, even the Holy Spirit, comes in to dwell in his heart. In Christ he has died to sin, and he is to reckon himself dead to sin but alive unto God through Jesus Christ our Lord.[7] He now has a new indwelling power to enable him to give up his sin.

B. "THERE IS SOMEONE I CANNOT FORGIVE."

Tell this one it is not a question of not being able to forgive, but of not being willing to forgive. Read to him the parable Jesus gave on the law of forgiveness as found in Matthew 18:21-35. The servant was forgiven a debt approximating $1,500,000, yet he would not forgive a fellow servant a debt equivalent to $15.00. God is willing to forgive a debt which is so great, surely an individual can forgive a fellow man a debt which in comparison is so small.

C. "I BELIEVE BUT I DON'T FEEL SAVED."

This is a most miserable predicament to be in, for the individual is never quite sure of salvation. One day there is glad assurance, but the next day it has disappeared. One day the

---

[5]Heb. 7:25.
[6]II Cor. 5:17.
[7]Rom. 6:11.

sun is shining, the sea of life is calm, and everything is lovely; but on the next the clouds are rolling in, the waves are angry and turbulent and there is no peace.

1. *Reason for Lack of Assurance.*

The reason often is that the person looks within rather than to Jesus, and gauges assurance of salvation upon feeling rather than upon faith. Nowhere does the Bible assure the believer that he will always feel on "top of the world," for our feelings are very often conditioned by what we eat, the amount of rest we have had, or the circumstances of the day. So one must never look for assurance of salvation to his feelings.

Someone has truly said: "If you look without, you are distressed; if you look within you are depressed; if you look to Him you are at rest." The believer must learn to look to Jesus at all times, under all circumstances, and in every situation.

2. *Some Questions Asked by the Seeker.*

a) Is God willing to keep the believer? Are there any promises in the Bible which definitely state that God is willing? There are many such promises.

Have our friend read John 17:11, where Jesus prayed: "And now I am no more in the world, but these are in the world, and I come to thee. Holy Father, keep through thine own name those whom thou hast given me, that they may be one, as we are." In this verse the Lord Jesus asks a very definite thing of the Father—that the Father will keep those whom He has given to the Lord Jesus. We may rest assured that every prayer of Christ has been heard and answered, for He always prayed in the will of God, and His prayers were always indicted of the Holy Spirit.

Then note another promise in this same chapter: "I pray not that thou shouldest take them out of the world, but that thou shouldest keep them from the evil [one]."[8] Here is another request of Christ for His Father to keep the disciples.

b) However, some troubled soul may say, "I know that Jesus prayed as you have read in these passages, but was not this prayer only for His immediate disciples?"

Tell this one that the question is a good one, and that it would seem the words of Christ only applied to the immediate disciples, but remind him of John 17:20: "Neither pray I for these alone, but for them also which shall believe on me through their word." These words of Christ ought to be sufficient to demonstrate to the one who lacks assurance that he is included also in the words of Christ.

Paul reminded the Roman Christians of their state before they came to Christ. They were "without strength"; they were "ungodly"; they were "sinners"; they were "enemies of God." When they were in this condition Christ died for them.[9] Then Paul reminded them that they were being kept saved by the life the Lord Jesus was now living.

But the things that were true of the Roman Christians were also true of each Christian today. Each one of us before we turned to Christ was "without strength," "ungodly," a sinner, and an enemy of God. But Christ has died for us and we are now kept saved by His life. We believe this because it is in God's Word and that gives assurance to the heart.

There is another wonderful promise in John's Gospel: "My sheep hear my voice, and I know them, and they follow me: and I give unto them eternal life; and they shall never perish, neither shall any man pluck them out of my hand.

---

[8]John 17:15.
[9]Rom. 5:6-10.

My Father which gave them me, is greater than all; and no man is able to pluck them out of my Father's hand."[10]

c) The disturbed inquirer may bring up another question: "If I am not to rely on my feelings for the assurance of salvation, how may I know that I am a believer?"

(1) Make it clear that God's Word is very definite and positive on the subject of salvation. This is the result of faith in the Person of the Lord Jesus Christ. It is not primarily faith in the work that Christ did on the cross, but faith in the Person who did the work. Salvation is the meeting of the sinner and the Saviour. The Bible uses the words *believe* and *confess* many times,[11] but never once is the individual told he must experience a certain kind of emotion or feeling in order to be saved.

(2) A second evidence of salvation is love for God and His Word. A genuine believer will realize that the Bible is God's Book, and that it contains food for his soul. It is God's love letter to him and he will desire to read it. Jesus said: "If a man love me, he will keep my words."[12]

John wrote in his First Epistle: "But whoso keepeth his word, in him verily is the love of God perfected: hereby know we that we are in him."[13]

(3) Another evidence of salvation is love for the brethren. John wrote: "We know that we have passed from death unto life, because we love the brethren."[14] "Whosoever believeth that Jesus is the Christ is born of God: and everyone that loveth him that begat loveth him also that is begotten of him."[15]

Some years ago a friend from a southern city came to

---

[10]John 10:27-29.
[11]John 3:16; Rom. 10:9, 10.
[12]John 14:23.
[13]I John 2:5.
[14]I John 3:14.
[15]I John 5:1.

visit me. He had with him a letter which he had recently received from his sister, who had been saved only a short time before. She had been a church member for some years, but because she had not known the Lord, she criticized her brother and his zeal for the Lord's work. She could not understand why he and the people in the little church could be so friendly with each other and love to be in each other's presence.

One day the Lord saved her, and this letter which my friend had received told him about the experience. She said she could now understand why real Christians loved to be together—it was because they all had the same kind of life. That is exactly what John was talking about.

(4) Then too, when one believes on Christ the blessed Holy Spirit comes into his heart to dwell. Because He takes up His abode we shall be conscious of His presence. One of the marks of the Holy Spirit's indwelling is that we desire to call God our Father. He establishes a new relationship. Paul wrote of this: "And because ye are sons, God hath sent forth the Spirit of his Son into your hearts, crying, Abba, Father."[16] "For ye have not received the spirit of bondage again to fear; but ye have received the Spirit of adoption, whereby we cry, Abba, Father. The Spirit itself beareth witness with our spirit, that we are the children of God."[17]

John also described this blessed truth: "And this is his commandment, That we should believe on the name of his Son Jesus Christ, and love one another, as he gave us commandment. And he that keepeth his commandments dwelleth in him, and he in him. And hereby we know that he abideth in us, by the Spirit which he hath given us."[18]

(5) Assurance of heart is the result of resting upon the

---

[16]Gal. 4:6.
[17]Rom. 8:15, 16.
[18]I John 3:23, 24.

truths in God's Word. When one is thus resting it will
make no difference how he may be feeling at the moment.
John wrote: "These things have I written unto you that believe on the name of the Son of God; that ye may know that
ye have eternal life, and that ye may believe on the name of
the Son of God."[19] It is *believe* and know, not *feel* and know.

D. "CHRISTIANS ARE SO INCONSISTENT."

Do not try to argue against this charge, but admit it.
There are hypocrites in the church, but there are many more
on the outside than in. Every good thing is counterfeited.
Dime-store jewelry is not counterfeited, but the genuine
stones in the expensive store next door may be. There are
many who claim to be Christians, and like the tares in the
parable[20] are almost like the wheat, but there is a difference
which eternity will reveal.

1. *Lack of Understanding*.

On the other hand, the person who will have nothing to
do with the church because he claims there are hypocrites
in it, does not understand that many at whom he is looking
are babes in Christ. He hears of one who is a Christian and
he begins to watch that life. When it does not measure up to
his estimation of the Christian life, he immediately criticizes
it because he does not understand a fundamental truth in
the Christian life: that a person is born into God's family
as a spiritual baby, not as a perfect adult Christian. Many
infantile characteristics may remain if the individual does
not grow in grace and in the knowledge of Christ. It must
be admitted that because many Christians do not study the
Bible and grow in knowledge they do not grow into mature
Christians. These are the ones at which the critic looks
when he passes judgment upon all Christians.

---

[19] I John 5:13.
[20] Matt. 13:24-30.

2. *May Be Only Excuse.*

After talking with this person the personal worker may feel that the existence of hypocrites in the church is not the real reason for his failure to come to Christ. It may lie deeper than that. That which he gives as a reason may be just an excuse. Try to get him to see this fact.

3. *Method of Handling.*

a) Endeavor to turn his attention to himself and his own condition. Show him that his own heart is deceitful above all things and desperately wicked, and that the Lord is the One who searches the heart.[21]

b) Show him too that every man must stand alone before God. He must answer for himself. There are many things we must do independently of others. We are born separately into this world, we die alone, and we stand before God alone. The flimsy excuse of another person's inconsistencies will not constitute a ground for righteousness before God. Paul wrote: "For they being ignorant of God's righteousness, and going about to establish their own righteousness, have not submitted themselves unto the righteousness of God."[22] "For not he that commendeth himself is approved, but whom the Lord commendeth."[23]

c) Judging others is not a way to escape judgment, but is the surest way to incur it. The Bible is very clear on this point. "Therefore thou art inexcusable, O man, whosoever thou art that judgest: for wherein thou judgest another, thou condemnest thyself; for thou that judgest doest the same things. But we are sure that the judgment of God is according to truth against them which commit such things. And thinkest thou this, O man, that judgest them which do such

---

[21]Jer. 17:9, 10.
[22]Rom. 10:3.
[23]II Cor. 10:18.

things, and doest the same, that thou shalt escape the judgment of God? Or despisest thou the riches of his goodness and forbearance and long-suffering; not knowing that the goodness of God leadeth thee to repentance? But after thy hardness and impenitent heart treasurest up unto thyself wrath against the day of wrath and revelation of the righteous judgment of God; who will render to every man according to his deeds: to them who by patient continuance in well doing seek for glory and honor and immortality, eternal life: but unto them that are contentious, and do not obey the truth, but obey unrighteousness, indignation and wrath, tribulation and anguish, upon every soul of man that doeth evil, of the Jew first and also of the Gentile: but glory, honor, and peace, to every man that worketh good, to the Jew first, and also to the Gentile: for there is no respect of persons with God."[24]

d) Show the critic that when the Lord calls His true Church to Himself to meet Him in the air, the hypocrites will all be left behind.[25] Only those whose names are in the Lamb's book of life will be in that group,[26] while the rest will have their place in the lake of fire which is the second death.[27] It is possible for one to have his name on the church roll without having it in the Lamb's book of life. Ask him if his name is in that book. If it is not, he will spend eternity with the hypocrites, for he will be one of them. Urge him to accept Christ, for it is better to spend a few years down here with some hypocrites and to be separated from them for all eternity, than to try to shun them down here for a few years, only to spend eternity in their company.

[24]Rom. 2:1-11.
[25]I Thess. 4:13-18.
[26]Rev. 21:27.
[27]Rev. 21:8; 22:15.

E. "WE ARE ALL HEADED FOR HEAVEN ALTHOUGH ALONG DIFFERENT ROADS."

This is a popular hope believed by many people. It is based on the thought that Heaven is the goal of all who are religious, and who are trying to do the best they can. God is thought to be the Father of all, and that there are many roads which lead into His presence.

1. *Sincerity Does Not Mean Salvation.*

If one is sincere in what he believes it does not make any difference what he believes, for all roads lead to God. This idea is expressed in a little poem, the author of which is unknown to the writer:

> All roads that lead to God are good;
>   What matters it, your faith or mine?
> All center at the goal divine
>   Of love's eternal brotherhood.
>
> Before the oldest book was writ,
>   Full many a prehistoric soul
> Arrived at that unchanging goal
>   Through changeless love which led to it.
>
> Though branch by branch proves withered wood,
>   The root is warm with precious wine.
> Then keep your faith, and leave me mine;
>   All roads that lead to God are good.

2. *Christ's Teaching.*

The Lord Jesus Christ did not teach this popular philosophy. Note some of His words which teach so plainly that He alone is the only way to Heaven.

"I am the way, the truth, and the life: no man cometh unto the Father, but by me."[28]

---

[28] John 14:6.

"I am the door of the sheep. All that ever came before me are thieves and robbers: but the sheep did not hear them. I am the door: by me if any man enter in, he shall be saved, and shall go in and out, and find pasture."[29]

"My sheep hear my voice, and I know them, and they follow me: and I give unto them eternal life; and they shall never perish, neither shall any man pluck them out of my hand. My father, which gave them me, is greater than all; and no man is able to pluck them out of my Father's hand. I and my Father are one."[30]

"I said therefore unto you, that ye shall die in your sins: for if ye believe not that I am he, ye shall die in your sins."[31]

3. *New Testament Writers.*

Writers of the New Testament have given the same truth. Following are a few of the many Scriptures, which state in various ways the fact that there is only one way into Heaven, and that is through the Lord Jesus Christ: "Neither is there salvation in any other: for there is none other name under heaven given among men, whereby we must be saved."[32] "Be it known unto you therefore, men and brethren, that through this man is preached unto you the forgiveness of sins: and by him all that believe are justified from all things, from which ye could not be justified by the law of Moses."[33] "For there is one God, and one mediator between God and men, the man Christ Jesus."[34] "For other foundation can no man lay than that is laid, which is Jesus Christ."[35] "For Christ also hath once suffered for sins, the just for the unjust,

---

[29]John 10:7-10.
[30]John 10:27-30.
[31]John 8:24.
[32]Acts 4:12.
[33]Acts 13:38, 39.
[34]I Tim. 2:5.
[35]I Cor. 3:11.

that he might bring us to God, being put to death in the flesh, but quickened by the Spirit."[36]

These Scriptures are sufficient to prove that there is only one way to Heaven. It is the straight and narrow way which leads unto life.[37] Any other way makes one a trespasser.

Paul reminded the Ephesian Christians that before they came to Christ they were dead in trespasses and sins.[38] They had been very religious as worshipers of the goddess Diana, but this very fact had made them trespassers, for they had been trying to get into Heaven some other way than that which God had ordained through Christ.

Dr. Harry Rimmer frequently gave an illustration of this truth which always delighted his audiences. It was an experience he had as a boy when he lived in a valley in California.

This particular summer he and his friends had been swimming each afternoon in the river which flowed to the west of the town. One afternoon they decided to swim in the river on the east of town, and the road to this river went by the orchard of a man named Paginni.

Paginni raised the finest apricots in the valley, and protected them vigorously. He had posted his orchard with "No Trespassing" signs. Every few feet along the road was one of these warnings. In addition he patrolled his ground carrying a double-barreled shotgun loaded with rock salt. At his heels trotted a vicious bulldog.

As this group of boys walked down the road, they were "much surprised" to note that Paginni's apricots were ripe. Their mouths watered for this lucious fruit. But every few feet they noticed one of the "No Trespassing" signs. Paginni

---

[36]I Peter 3:18.
[37]Matt. 7:14.
[38]Eph. 2:1.

had had trouble before with these boys, and he had determined not to let them sample his fruit this season.

One boy looked at the other and after laboriously spelling out "No Trespassing," said, "I wonder what that means?"

No one seemed to know, but they came to the conclusion that it probably meant, "Keep Out."

That disconcerting fact, however, did not lessen their desire for some of Paginni's choice apricots.

As they slowly walked along, they came to a small space where there was no sign. This was their opportunity for appropriating some of the fruit. So charging Harry's young brother to stay outside and warn them if Paginni should come, assuring him that they would magnanimously reward him with apricots, they climbed the fence and were soon enjoying the fruit. The smaller boys stayed on the ground, but the bigger boys climbed into the trees. Harry, being the leader of the gang, chose the best tree, and climbed to the top where the best apricots were hanging. He ate his fill, and then decided to take some with him for eating after his swim. So tying his shirt tails around him, he very carefully stuffed his shirt with the tree-ripened fruit.

But a disastrous thing had happened in the meantime. The "watchman" who had been stationed on the road, and whose sole responsibility was to warn his friends if Mr. Paginni entered the orchard, knowing the integrity of his companions was not to be trusted, concluded that if he were to enjoy his fill of apricots he must get them for himself. So he left his post of duty and climbed the fence.

He was enjoying the fruit, and he did not see Paginni enter the orchard. When Paginni was noticed, the boys let out a yell, climbed over the fence, and headed for the river.

Harry started down as carefully as possible, for he did not

wish to damage the fruit in his shirt. But noticing that
Paginni was rapidly getting closer, he threw caution to the
winds, and slid down as fast as he could. The fruit was
mashed against his chest and squeezed out around his col-
lar. Mr. Paginni, realizing he would not capture his prey,
stopped, took aim and fired. His aim was excellent. Harry
let out a yell, dropped to the ground, leaped the fence, and
ran to the river. He dove in and swam to the other side.
Then he warmed the cool sand for at least one quarter of a
mile as he moved from spot to spot to relieve the stinging
of the rock salt.

Darkness had fallen when he arrived home. His little
brother had preceded him by about an hour and had informed his mother of the happenings of the afternoon. Supper was over and his mother was doing the dishes. After he
had eaten his supper, Harry said to his mother, "Maw, what
does 'No Trespassing' mean?"

His mother, being a very wise woman, did not stop her
work but merely replied, "Son, I think you know."

"No Trespassing" means "Keep Out." The owner of a
piece of property has a perfect right to insist that no one
come onto his land without his permission, and if a person
does not secure that permission he is a trespasser.

God has the same right. He has said that no one can get
into His Heaven except over the way He has provided.
That way is through the Lord Jesus Christ. Every other
way makes the seeker a trespasser.

F. "THE CHRISTIAN LIFE IS TOO HARD."

This is an objection sometimes given when the claims of
Christ are pressed upon an individual.

1. *Complaints.*

He may say, "I've tried the Christian life but have always

failed." "There are too many things to give up." "It is O.K. for old people and children but not for young people." "It takes all the joy out of life."

2. *How To Deal.*

a) Tell this individual that the Christian life, the genuine Christian life, is not behaviorism but a new life with new desires, new attitudes, new purposes, and new destiny. It is Christ in the individual who is living out His life in the believer.

b) The Bible gives the true picture of life. According to it every person is either saved or lost, either a child of God or a child of the Devil, either on his way to Heaven or on his way to Hell. Ask him to which group he belongs.

c) Show this person the folly of rejecting Christ, for it means that he will die in his sins;[39] that he is now living under the wrath of God;[40] and day by day he is storing up wrath against the day of wrath and revelation of the righteous judgment of God;[41] for he is despising the riches of the goodness and long-suffering of God.[42] Impress upon this one that he is only one heart-beat from eternity and that if he were to die in his sins he would experience immediate suffering.[43] Tell him the Bible says that there is a way which seemeth right unto a man but the end thereof are the ways of death,[44] that sin always pays wages which is death.[45]

d) Show him, on the other hand, that there is forgiveness

---

[39] John 8:24.
[40] John 3:36.
[41] Rom. 2:5.
[42] Rom. 2:4.
[43] Luke 16:23.
[44] Prov. 14:12.
[45] Rom. 6:23.

of sin through Christ,[46] that Christ died for him to bring
him to God.[47]

G. "WHAT ABOUT THE BACKSLIDER; DOES HE NOT LOSE HIS SALVATION?"

1. *Meaning of Term.*

The backslider is a child of God who has fallen into sin.
The Scripture has several illustrations of this condition,
among them David,[48] and Peter.[49] Both of these men knew
God, but both of them went off into sin. David committed
adultery, and then instigated murder. Peter denied his
Lord with cursing and swearing, claiming that he never
knew Christ. Paul had to deal with some cases of backslid-
ing in the Corinthian church.[50]

2. *Restoration or Salvation?*

Does the backslider need to be saved again? Does he
lose his salvation when he sins? Some think so, and stress
a new act of salvation. The writer is of the conviction, however, that the child of God does not lose his salvation, but
his fellowship.

The prophet Nathan did not approach David on the basis
of his need of salvation, but of confession and forgiveness.
David's prayer of confession and his resultant forgiveness
are recorded in Psalms 51 and 32.

Peter was not told that he would need to be saved over
again, but that when he was "turned again" (Greek), he was
to strengthen the brethren.[51]

---

[46]Acts 13:38.
[47]I Peter 3:18.
[48]II Sam. 11–12.
[49]Luke 22:31-34; Mark 14:66-72.
[50]I Cor. 3:1-4; 5:1.
[51]Luke 22:32.

Paul did not intimate that the one who was guilty of incest had lost his salvation, but that he needed the discipline of the church. This led to his restoration.[52]

3. *The Lord Is Seeking Him.*

These cases bring home the truth that the Lord is seeking the backslider. He sometimes seeks him with the chastening rod;[53] He sometimes seeks him through the rebuke of fellow saints;[54] and He sometimes seeks him through direct appeal.[55]

4. *The Lord Desires To Keep Him.*

The Lord's desire to deliver and to keep for Himself those who drift from Him is illustrated in the deliverance of Lot from the city of Sodom,[56] and in the story of the prodigal son.[57]

5. *The Lord Is Praying for the Backslider.*

He said He would pray for Peter;[58] and John said: "If any man sin we have an advocate with the Father, Jesus Christ the righteous."[59]

6. *The Christian Accepts Backslider into Fellowship.*

The spiritual Christian is urged by Paul to restore the one who has been overtaken in a fault.[60]

7. *The Responsibility of the Backslider.*

The backslider's responsibility is to repent and confess.[61] Forgiveness and restoration to fellowship are promised by God.

---

[52]II Cor. 2:1-8.
[53]Luke 15:11-16; I Cor. 5:5; Heb. 12:5-14.
[54]II Sam. 12:1-7; Gal. 6:1.
[55]Isa. 1:18; Hosea 14:4, 5.
[56]Gen. 19:1-16.
[57]Luke 15:11-24.
[58]Luke 22:31-34.
[59]I John 2:1.
[60]Gal. 6:1.
[61]I John 1:9.

H. "RELIGION IS ALL FOOLISHNESS."

Agree with the speaker of this objection. It is true to the Scripture. This will startle the objector.

Paul wrote: "For the preaching of the cross is to them that perish foolishness; but unto us which are saved it is the power of God. For it is written, I will destroy the wisdom of the wise, and will bring to nothing the understanding of the prudent. Where is the wise? where is the scribe? where is the disputer of this world? hath not God made foolish the wisdom of this world? For after that in the wisdom of God the world by wisdom knew not God, it pleased God by the foolishness of preaching to save them that believe. For the Jews require a sign, and the Greeks seek after wisdom: but we preach Christ crucified, unto the Jews a stumbling block, and unto the Greeks foolishness. But unto them which are called, both Jews and Greeks, Christ the power of God, and the wisdom of God."[62]

"The world by its wisdom knew not God." How true that statement is! Religion is the way in which men seek for God. Christianity is the truth of God seeking men,[63] and that is very different.

Paul wrote again: "But the natural man receiveth not the things of the Spirit of God: for they are foolishness unto him: neither can he know them, because they are spiritually discerned."[64]

If the things of the Spirit of God are foolishness to a person, it is proof that that one is lost.

I. "GOD IS TOO GOOD TO SEND A POOR SINNER TO HELL."

The truth is that God has done everything necessary to keep the sinner out of Hell. If he goes there, it will be because he has chosen to go there.

---

[62]I Cor. 1:18-24.
[63]Luke 19:10.
[64]I Cor. 2:14

Dr. R. A. Torrey preached a sermon in his evangelistic campaigns years ago entitled, "God's Blockade of the Road to Hell." In it he pointed out the many blockades God has put in a man's way to Hell. Some of them are: "The Bible and Its Teaching"; "A Mother's Prayers"; "A Mother's Holy Influence and a Mother's Teaching"; "The Sermons That We Hear"; "A Sunday School Teacher's Influence"; "A Kind Word"; "The Holy Spirit and His Work"; "The Cross." If a man goes to Hell, it will be because he has paid no attention to the many blockades God has put in his way.

The lake of fire, the place of everlasting punishment, was prepared by God for the Devil and his angels.[65] There is no intimation that it was prepared for any other group of people than those mentioned by Jesus. However, Jesus said that those on His left hand in the judgment of the nations would be sent to the place of eternal punishment.

The apostle Paul wrote: "And to you who are troubled rest with us, when the Lord Jesus shall be revealed from heaven with his mighty angels, in flaming fire taking vengeance on them that know not God, and that obey not the gospel of our Lord Jesus Christ: who shall be punished with everlasting destruction from the presence of the Lord, and from the glory of his power; when he shall come to be glorified in his saints, and to be admired in all them that believe (because our testimony among you was believed) in that day."[66] The basis of judgment in this passage of Scripture is that the recipients of judgment are those who have not known God, and who have not obeyed the Gospel of the Lord Jesus Christ.

The Book of the Revelation gives a vivid picture of the Great White Throne judgment, when the dead stand before God and the books are opened. Each person in this scene

---

[65] Matt. 25:41, 46.
[66] II Thess. 1:7-9.

will be judged according to his works. Salvation is not the question but the degrees of punishment to be meted out. The last verse of this section is: "And whosoever was not found written in the book of life was cast into the lake of fire."[67]

Those who go to the lake of fire are sent there because their names are not written in the Lamb's book of life. Only the names of those who have acknowledged Jesus Christ as God's Son and their Saviour are in this book.

The objector who maintains that God is too good to send a sinner to Hell has not reckoned with the fact that Jesus Christ is the Lamb of God who came to take away the sin of the world.[68] The sin question was taken care of at Calvary, now it is the Son question. Those who reject the Son will not see life, but the wrath of God must abide on them.[69]

No one can reject God's Son with impunity. God will be severe on the enemies of His Son. John wrote: "Whosoever denieth the Son, the same hath not the Father."[70] "He that honoreth not the Son honoreth not the Father which hath sent him."[71]

QUESTIONS AND EXERCISES

1. What should the personal worker determine regarding the person who claims he cannot give up his sins?
2. Give some reasons why people do not want to give up their sins.
3. List the Scripture verses which prove God is able to cleanse from all sin.
4. Why should one not look to his feelings for the assurance of salvation?

---

[67]Rev. 20:11-15.
[68]John 1:29.
[69]John 3:36.
[70]I John 2:23.
[71]John 5:23.

5. Give some scriptural evidences of salvation.
6. How can one account for the inconsistencies of Christians?
7. Why cannot the objector who says there are too many hypocrites in the church hide behind them?
8. Prove it is not true that all faiths lead to God.
9. Give the Scripture which teaches Christ is the only way to God the Father.
10. Why do some claim the Christian life is too hard? How would you deal with them?
11. Give several reasons why it is folly to reject Christ.
12. Who is a backslider?
13. Give some Biblical illustrations of backsliders.
14. What is the backslider's responsibility?
15. What is the difference between religion and Christianity?
16. Can the world by its wisdom know God? Prove from Scripture.
17. Is the lake of fire burning now? What Scripture teaches this?
18. Who will be put into it?
19. Name some of the blockades God has placed in a person's way.
20. Why will God be severe on the enemies of His Son?

The Cults

A. MEANING OF CULT.

IN ITS MOST GENERAL SENSE the word *cult* signifies any system of worship. Under this definition Christianity can be called a cult, as also Mohammedanism, Buddhism, and all the other religions of the world. There are, of course, differences between all these religions and Christianity which make our faith stand out unique from all other systems. The chief difference may be expressed in one statement, namely, that while religions of the world are attempts of men to reach out to God, Christianity reveals God reaching down to men. It is not difficult to see how this difference affects the hope of salvation.

We are not concerned with this general meaning of the word *cult*. We are rather using it with a more specialized connotation, referring to those systems which arise within the orbit of professed Christianity, claiming to be the true Christianity, while at the same time destroying the essential message of our faith. They are not to be confused with the evangelical denominations which, while differing on certain matters of doctrine and practice, yet basically hold the essential Christian truth. We are thinking more of heretical sects who trade with the name "Christian," but depart from the central truths. There may indeed be borderline cases where it is difficult to determine whether a group may be called a denomination or a heretical sect, and in some instances the decision will depend largely on one's background. In one book dealing with departures from orthodox Christianity the Plymouth Brethren were dealt with as a cult, thoroughly heretical, whereas many of us regard them as among the most faithful of our evangelical groups. This will indicate that in some cases we shall have to use great care in passing judgment.

B. Various Ways Cults Arise.

1. *Perversion of Truth.*

In some quarters there has been a gradual perversion of Christian truth, going along with multiplied accretions of falsehood which tend to bury what truth remains. The outstanding example of this is Roman Catholicism. In this system there is much truth. Most of us could recite in unison with Roman Catholics the Apostles' Creed. On the other hand, so much of the truth found in the Roman system is perverted and given false expression, while there have been added many dogmas which have no place in Biblical Christianity, and which go far to annul the residue of truth. I have dealt with this in my little book, *The Bible and the Roman Church.*[1]

2. *Deletion of Scriptures.*

Another means by which cults come into being is a process of subtraction. Men who seem to have a prejudice against the supernatural and the miraculous simply strain out these elements from the record, leaving us with a denatured Christianity which is nothing more than Naturalism and Humanism. This is what we have in the cult of Modernism—a word which, by the way, has been greatly overused, too often signifying nothing more than a variation from the doctrinal

---

[1]J. C. Macaulay, *The Bible and the Roman Church* (Chicago 10: Moody Press).

position of the person speaking! There are many degrees
between the extreme fundamentalist and the thorough-
going modernist, and we need to be careful that we do not
malign a brother who holds with us the great essentials of
the Christian faith, but who differs from us on some matters
of Biblical criticism, or perhaps is guilty of holding a different view of eschatology. We certainly should not encourage
any tendency to diminish the supernatural content of our
Christian faith, but on the other hand, we should not falsely
accuse men of this heresy who are far from guilty.

3. *Undue Stress on Certain Truths.*

Cults arise in yet a third way. Some aspect of truth, perhaps a neglected aspect, is laid hold of and raised to undue
prominence, being made the peg upon which a whole system
is hung. An example of this is Jehovah's Witnesses, who
have laid hold upon certain aspects of prophecy, having
given these their own interpretations and built their whole
doctrine around these false interpretations. Before they are
through they have denied the deity of Christ, the Biblical
teaching of the atonement, the resurrection, and the entire
doctrine of grace, but the prophecy is their starting point.

4. *False Unity.*

Yet again, some object to the exclusive claims of Biblical
Christianity, and affirm that light has come from many quarters. These make an attempt to unify the various beams of
light, as they regard them. Confucius, Mohammed, Moses,
Jesus, Socrates, are indiscriminately brought together as
channels of revelation from God. Thus a system is worked
out which makes room for them all, and this is regarded as
the true Christianity. Such a system is Baha'i with its strange
mingling of philosophies and mysteries.

5. *Fanaticism.*

We need hardly speak of those who play on the gullibility

of the public, building religious systems around themselves
with the spice of strong emotional content. For instance,
the religion of Father Divine is entirely self-centered. One
is amazed that he has any following at all, and one wonders
what will happen to the whole structure when he goes the
way of all flesh, thus demonstrating that after all he, too,
was but a man.

C. How Cults Prosper.

A more serious problem than how cults arise is how they
prosper. Let us consider a few reasons for their rapid spread.

1. *Ignorance of Christian Doctrine.*

The first reason that I should offer is the ignorance of so
many professing Christians with regard to Christian doctrine. It is noticeable that the vast majority of converts to
the heretical cults are drawn from those who are either in
churches where Biblical doctrine is little taught, or from
those who are simply on the fringe of the church, and do not
sufficiently expose themselves to its teaching. Not being
grounded and settled in the faith, they are virgin soil for the
seed of falsehood, skillfully sown.

2. *Trained Representatives of the Cults.*

A second reason is the trained salesmanship of the representatives of the cults. Whether they be Mormons or Jehovah's Witnesses or whatever they be, they are thoroughly
instructed in the particular doctrines of their sect, and well
trained in presenting these doctrines. In many cases modern
equipment is freely used and the representatives are instructed in the most approved psychological approaches.

3. *Zeal of the Cults.*

A third reason for the success of the cults is the zeal with
which their propaganda is pressed forward. In many of
them there is special merit in propagating the faith, and in

some cases it is even a matter of salvation. Certainly their
zeal ought to challenge us who are entrusted with the Gospel of the grace of God.

4. *Emphasis on Neglected Truth.*

A fourth reason for success is the fact that they frequently
put their first emphasis on some neglected aspect of truth.
Many, for instance, who have had no instruction in the prophetic Scriptures are introduced to them in the perverted
forms of Jehovah's Witnesses or Seventh-Day Adventists.
Believing that they have been deprived of the truth, they
quickly embrace the cult which seems to offer it to them.

5. *Cults Carry Christian Name.*

A fifth reason is that these cults carry the Christian name,
which gives them a certain respectability in the eyes of the
public. There are great multitudes in America outside the
immediate influence of the churches who still call themselves Christians and think of America as a Christian nation.
Whatever comes, then, with the Christian label is regarded
with some degree of respect.

6. *Satan-blinded Minds.*

A sixth reason is given us in the words of the apostle Paul:
"If our gospel be hid, it is hid to them that are lost: in whom
the god of this world hath blinded the minds of them which
believe not, lest the light of the glorious gospel of Christ,
who is the image of God, should shine unto them."[2] We
must not be unmindful of the activity of the powers of darkness. In many cases the most effectual way to keep men
from the truth is to feed them with falsehood which has some
appearance of truth.

7. *Refusal of Truth.*

Yet a seventh reason, also drawn from the teaching of the
apostle Paul, is that those who refuse the truth fall an easy

---
[2]II Cor. 4:3, 4.

prey to the lie.[3] Here is the operation of a spiritual law, and it certainly is amazing how many have turned away from the truth of the Gospel only to become ardent disciples of some heresy shortly after.

These reasons constitute a real challenge to the Christian. What a responsibility rests upon the church to teach sound doctrine, and to train its people in the sacred task of taking the Gospel to others! What a call there is for God's people to be stirred out of our lethargy, and at least to match the zeal of those who are themselves deceived, and therefore are deceiving others! Then, too, we have the call to prayer, which is our combat weapon against the powers of darkness.

D. How To Distinguish False Cults.

Our next question is—How can we distinguish false cults from true Christianity? I am going to suggest five tests which we may apply to any system presented to us.

1. *The Test of Authority.*

We recognize the Scriptures of the Old and New Testaments as our authority in matters of faith and practice. Most of the cults which we have in mind profess to accept the Bible, but one sure mark of their heretical nature is that it is a matter of the Bible plus, or the Bible minus. What I mean is that they add to or take from the Bible in plain defiance of the warning given at the end of the Holy Scriptures.[4] In Mormonism the recognized authority is the Bible plus *The Book of Mormon*. In Christian Science it is the Bible plus *Science and Health with Key to the Scriptures*. In Roman Catholicism it is the Bible plus tradition, plus the decrees of the church councils, plus the Papal bulls. On the other hand, with modernism it is the Bible minus all which does not appeal to the modern mind.

---

[3] II Thess. 2:10, 11.
[4] Rev. 22:18, 19.

2. *Their View of the Nature of God.*

We can ask them several questions. What do they believe with regard to the personality of God? This question will find Christian Science on the short end, for in this system the personality of God is completely rejected. Again, what do they believe concerning the transcendence of God? Is He over all? This will find out all the cults which have pantheistic leanings, and here also Christian Science stands condemned. Again, what is their attitude to the Holy Trinity? Here Jehovah's Witnesses stand forth as the enemies of the truth, for if there is one doctrine which they hate it is the doctrine of the Trinity. Once more we may ask, what do they believe about the righteousness of God? There are those who insist much on the love of God and His fatherly disposition toward men but completely ignore His invincible and inflexible righteousness. This weakens their position all along the line. All kinds of universalism are condemned on this score.

3. *Their View of the Person of Christ.*

How do they stand with regard to His deity, His pre-existence, His humanity, His death and resurrection? This question discovers the failure of many of them. It is exactly in this sphere that many heresies have arisen all through the history of the church. Jehovah's Witnesses have resurrected an ancient heresy to the effect that Jesus was a created being of angelic nature, and as such was entrusted with all other creation; that in the incarnation He completely lost His angelic nature and was nothing but a man; that when He died, that was the end of the man Jesus. But somehow this one who had lost His angel nature in coming to earth, and had now lost His human nature in dying, was exalted to the divine nature. There was no resurrection, but a miraculous dissolution of the body into gases, unless, per-

haps, it was miraculously removed to some corner of the
universe to be brought forth to view during the Millennium.
This is an amazing example of what heresy can do with the
Person of Christ.

4. *Their View of Sin.*

Is sin a reality? The Bible says, "Yes"; Christian Science
says, "No." Does sin involve guilt? The Bible says, "Yes";
the materialist says, "No," while the modernist quibbles.
Does sin affect God, and make any change in His attitude
to men? The Bible says, "Yes"; but most of the cults give a
noncommittal answer. Where there is a low view of sin,
one had better not trust his soul to that system.

5. *Their View of Salvation.*

The fifth test that I would suggest concerns the way of
salvation. The Bible way of salvation is: "By grace are ye
saved through faith; and that not of yourselves: it is the
gift of God: not of works, lest any man should boast."[5] The
heretical cults are almost universally autosoteric to a greater
or lesser degree; that is, they teach self-salvation in some
form. Christian Science, for instance, teaches that salvation
is by the diligent ridding of the mind of the error that there
is anything from which to be saved. Jehovah's Witnesses
teach a distinctly autosoteric doctrine. According to them
the death of Christ secures for us only a chance to prove
ourselves. So we might go through the list. They all fall
short of the Bible way of salvation.[6]

It is not the purpose of this book to expound the cults.
While this is usually part of a course in personal evangelism,

[5]Eph. 2:8, 9.
[6]My collaborator, Dr. Robert Belton, suggests a sixth test of the cults,
namely, their view of Creation. Views of Creation range all the way from
a complete sovereign act of God to a thorough-going materialistic evolution.
Any view of the world and its origin which transfers the glory of Creation
from God to matter is decidedly heretical, and systems which adopt such
views cannot be regarded with favor by evangelical Christians.

it is really a special subject, the inclusion of which would necessitate too much enlargement of the present volume. The work which I have used in class is that by Van Baalen, entitled *The Chaos of Cults.*[7]

E. How To Deal with Members of Cults.

Meeting members of these various cults is no easy task, especially if they have been strongly indoctrinated.

1. *Do Not Argue.*

Those who embrace these false systems frequently become very determined and are closed to reason. On the other hand, the temptation for the Christian worker is to argue. That generally antagonizes more than it helps.

2. *Live Life of Holiness.*

The Christian's best answer to all falsehood is the truth demonstrated in a life of holiness. Many have turned to the cults because they saw little reality in those who called themselves Christians. If our lives make it evident that Christ is real to us in all situations, we shall be giving a testimony stronger than all argument or disputation. Above all, we must show the love of Christ.

3. *Pray Much.*

Then we have the mighty weapon of prayer. Here is where most of us are defective. Prayer is a test of patience, of endurance, of faith, and we do not care for such tests. When we pray, we are undermining the hold of the powers of darkness on the lives of men. When we pray, God works. We ought to pray that God will bring those who are caught in these snares into situations in which their false systems fail them. Then they will be ready to hear the Gospel of God's grace.

---

[7] J. K. Van Baalen, *The Chaos of Cults* (Grand Rapids: Eerdmans Publishing Co.).

4. *Use Word of God.*

When the time comes to speak, it will be well to confine oneself to fundamental matters, and let the Bible speak. Our opinions are of no value. Our interpretations are no more valid than those of the one to whom we are witnessing. Ask the Holy Spirit to be the Interpreter.

If the cult in question plays down the sin question, let the Bible speak on that subject, using such Scriptures as Romans 3:10, 23; I John 1:8-10; James 2:10; Galatians 3:10; Isaiah 64:6. If it denies judgment, turn to Matthew 25:41, 46; II Thessalonians 1:7-9; Hebrews 9:27; Acts 17:30, 31. If it is universalistic, apply John 14:6; Acts 4:12; I Timothy 2:5. In other words, discover the basic weakness of the cult, and bring the sharp weapon of the Word to bear upon it at that point. If the Scriptures offered in Lessons 16 to 21 have been mastered, they will be found to meet the weak spots of all the false systems.

QUESTIONS AND EXERCISES

1. What is the most general meaning of the word *cult*, and how does this differ from the sense in which we use it?
2. List and explain the different ways in which cults arise, giving examples.
3. Name and explain seven factors in the remarkable prosperity of many of the cults.
4. Write a theme on "How the Cults Present a Challenge to Evangelical Christians."
5. What tests should be applied to determine the truth or falsehood of any system?
6. Make a list of cults which profess to follow the Bible but offer other "authorities."
7. State briefly the Christology of Jehovah's Witnesses.
8. What is meant by *autosoteric?* Give examples in various cults.

How To Deal with Roman Catholics

WHILE THIS WORK cannot deal particularly with the various cults, there are two large groups commanding our attention, because we are likely to be brought into contact with them, and in dealing with them we need much wisdom and grace. I refer to Roman Catholics and Jews. Concerning both of these groups, I would urge that we completely rid our hearts of all prejudice. If we suspect every Roman Catholic we meet of plotting to destroy our liberty, and if we think of every Jew as ready to strike a hard bargain, we are not likely to do them much good. On the other hand, if we love them as souls for whom Christ died, and consistently cultivate the practice of seeing their virtues, we shall be able to approach them with a frankness and a friendliness which will disarm any prejudice that may exist on their side. Remember that personal evangelism is a matter of the heart even more than of the head. We may learn the technique, but if we have not love, we have failed before we begin. Now let us consider a few hints for dealing with Roman Catholics.

A. KNOW THEIR BELIEFS.

Be sure that you know what Roman Catholics believe. If you are unaware of their position you are definitely handicapped in making an appropriate presentation of the Gospel. Almost every basic doctrine of the Christian faith which you may present, they will claim to believe. Unless, therefore, you have learned the weak spots in their armor, you will not know what arrow to use and where to aim it. I have tried to present the Roman position accurately in my little book already mentioned, *The Bible and the Roman Church*.[1] I have quoted their own authorities, but have sought to make the presentation nonacademic. There are many other works which set forth the doctrine of the Roman Church in comparison with the Gospel of the grace of God, and the personal worker should certainly secure some such help in coming to an understanding of those whom he desires to point to Christ.

B. Be Accurate in Use of Terms.

My second suggestion logically follows the first—be accurate in your statements. For instance, do not speak about the Immaculate Conception when you mean the Virgin Birth. The Immaculate Conception is the phrase they use to express their belief that Mary, the mother of our Lord, was conceived in her mother's womb free from original sin. This is one of "the prerogatives of Mary," as they say. The Virgin Birth, of course, deals with the birth of our Lord by means of a miraculous conception.

Another example may be drawn from the practice of indulgences. Many Protestants believe that indulgences are permissions to sin, and to make such a statement to a Roman Catholic immediately reveals one's ignorance and disqualifies him from further usefulness with that Roman Catholic. Indulgences have to do with the mitigating of temporal punishment due to sin, and are intended to reduce the term

---

[1] J. C. Macaulay, *The Bible and the Roman Church* (Chicago 10: Moody Press).

of one's sufferings in purgatory after death. They are usually
granted by the Pope on the basis of the merits of the blood
of Christ, plus the merits of the Virgin and the Saints. They
are bestowed in return for meritorious deeds of charity, or
devotion, or voluntary penance.

C. USE ROMAN CATHOLIC VERSION.

In the third place, I suggest that the personal worker use
a Roman Catholic version of the Bible. They are taught
that Protestant versions are perverted and corrupted. We
ought to show them, therefore, that we are not afraid of
their versions. It is true that Roman Catholic versions carry
Roman Catholic footnotes which sometimes offset the clear
sense of the text. Nevertheless, the text is there, and although there are a few renderings which we might dispute,
they are not sufficient to obscure the Gospel. The official
Bible of the Roman Catholic Church is the Latin Vulgate.
Therefore, their English versions are made from the Latin—
not, however, without some reference to the original languages. There are two editions which one may use: the
Douay, which for a long time was the recognized English
Roman Catholic version, and a more recent edition of the
New Testament prepared under the patronage of the Episco-
pal Committee of the Confraternity of Christian Doctrine.
I believe it is generally referred to as the Confraternity
Edition. It bears the *Imprimatur* of the Bishop of Paterson
and the *Nihil Obstat* of three clergymen, in addition to the
approval of Cardinal Tisserant. One will find it in many
respects an excellent translation. It is especially strong in
the Epistle to the Hebrews, where there is much insistence
on the sacrifice of Christ being once for all.[2]

---

[2]*See*, for instance, Heb. 7:27.

D. Avoid Slanderous Statements.

A fourth point to remember is to avoid all slanderous statements concerning their church. The history of the Roman Church has no lack of very dark blots. One could very easily pick out a number of Popes for condemnation, or make a case against the Roman Church as continually dabbling in politics, or show how it had sponsored bitter and bloody persecution, or denounce its lofty pretensions. None of that, however, would incline a Roman Catholic to listen to the message of the Gospel. It would only antagonize him. After all, our business is not to inquire into the vices of the Roman Church, but to point the individual to a present and living Saviour.

E. Respect the Virgin Mary.

The fifth point, like the fourth, is of a negative nature. By no means speak disrespectfully of the Virgin Mary. The Roman Church has certainly exalted her unduly, but that does not justify our assuming an antagonistic attitude toward her. We refrain from calling her the mother of God as Roman Catholics do, but we can very well use the language of Elizabeth and refer to her as the mother of our Lord.[3] A proper display of respect for the virgin mother will go a long way to disarm Roman Catholics who believe that we actually despise her, and I am afraid some Protestants have given them good reason for believing so. What we desire to do is to center the thoughts of our Roman Catholic friends on the sufficiency of Christ. We do not need to minimize the honor of Mary to do so.

F. Take Common Ground.

If we emphasize our points of difference, there is little likelihood of our finding a common meeting place at the

---

[3]Luke 1:43.

feet of Christ. It is true that before we are finished some
of our differences will be brought out into bold relief, but
make it clear that we hold much in common. Try them on
the inspiration of the Bible, the Holy Trinity, the deity of
Christ, His death for our sins, and His resurrection, the
personality of the Holy Spirit, the second coming of Christ,
eternal life, and judgment. You will find that they will go
a long way with you on these points. Having once laid a
foundation of common belief, it will not be so difficult to
deal with some of the differences which affect the way of
salvation.

G. MATTERS TO EMPHASIZE.

My seventh suggestion would be concerning the matters
that we must emphasize. I would say they are four in number:

a) Show that salvation may be had *now*.[4] Almost universally they believe that salvation is something which you receive after this life.

b) Emphasize salvation *apart from works*.[5] Their whole
way of salvation is by works, while, of course, they do not
deny the redeeming work of Christ.

c) Point out the Biblical doctrine of *assurance*.[6] Their
system offers them no assurance.

d) Insist on going *directly to Christ*.[7] They are directed
to intermediaries such as the Virgin Mary, the Saints, and the
priest.

These are the four points at which the weakness of the
Roman position becomes most evident. We should approach
these points carefully and tenderly. They will have their

---

[4]John 5:24; John 6:47; etc.
[5]Rom. 4:4, 5; Eph. 2:8, 9; Titus 3:4-7; etc.
[6]John 10:27-29; I John 5:13; Rom. 10:9-13; etc.
[7]John 14:6; I Tim. 2:5; Heb. 7:25; etc.

objections. For instance, they will say that the doctrine of present salvation tends to induce careless living, or that salvation apart from works is immoral, or that you cannot know that you are saved till after you die, or that they are unworthy to go directly to Christ; but hold them to the Scriptures, and trust the Holy Spirit to convince them of the truth. Let all be done in love, and with much prayer.

Questions and Exercises

1. How would you differentiate between the doctrines of the Virgin Birth and the Immaculate Conception? Why was the latter doctrine propounded?
2. Write out a brief explanation of the Roman Catholic system of indulgences.
3. What is meant by the *Imprimatur* and the *Nihil Obstat*?
4. Why do we call Mary the mother of our Lord, yet refuse to call her the mother of God?
5. List and explain the four main points of emphasis in presenting the Gospel to Roman Catholics.

LESSON 23

The Jew

A. Preparing To Deal with the Jew.

1. *Develop Right Heart Attitude.*

Preparation for dealing with Jews concerning their relationship to Jesus Christ must begin with the heart. So long as we have any disposition to be a Jew-baiter, we disqualify for this task.

a) It may be argued that Jew-baiting was a medieval practice, and has no place in our enlightened twentieth century, and especially in free America. So far as open persecution is concerned, this may be true. The disposition, however, is not so uncommon as one might wish. Such signs as, "For Gentiles Only," seen not infrequently, indicate that the barrier is not completely broken down. In many quarters where complete ostracism is not enforced, the Jew is, nevertheless, *persona non grata*. Even among Christians there is frequently a disposition to exaggerate some of the more unpleasant Jewish propensities, with rarely a word of commendation for the finer qualities of that race.

b) If we are to win them, we must first be won ourselves to a completely new point of view, and learn to regard the Jews in the light of their need, and their privilege. We may not treat them as a God-forsaken race in the face of the apostolic statement, "Hath God cast away his people? God forbid."[1]

---

[1] Rom. 11:1.

224

2. Understand Them.

A further step in preparation for dealing with Jews has to do with our understanding of them. It would be well for all who undertake to witness to Jews to read a good history of that people, beginning with Abraham right down to modern times.[2] See them as chosen of God, as God's witness in the midst of heathen nations. See them in their trials and their sufferings, in their failures and their judgments. See them with their sense of divine calling, yet under the heel of their persecutor. See them scattered to the ends of the earth, refusing to be absorbed, hated and feared, the objects of contempt, abuse, ridicule, the sport of their oppressors. See them driven from country to country, crowded into their ghettos, massacred at the whim of tyrants, and all this at the hands of those who called themselves Christians. These centuries of insecurity, persecution, and oppression can certainly go far to explain those characteristics which are so noted against them, but which need not be enumerated here. We might call them psychological sicknesses, induced by the treatment meted out to them in nations that were called Christian.

3. Recognize Admirable Traits.

Not only should we understand the cause of the less pleasing qualities in the Jew, but we should fully recognize many admirable traits, which they have in common, and as individuals. Not only are they shrewd businessmen, but in the arts and the sciences they have made notable contributions. In statesmanship, they are farseeing, and with all this, they have abounding energy and great determination.

4. Appreciate Their Spiritual Contribution.

[2]Cecil Roth, A Bird's-eye View of Jewish History (Cincinnati 2: Union of American Hebrew Congregations). Paul Goodman, A History of the Jews (Cleveland: World Publishing Co.). Lady Magnus, Outlines of Jewish History (Philadelphia: Jewish Publication Co. of America).

Despite their shortcomings and their failures, we should not forget that they were the agent through whom God gave and preserved the revelation of Himself to a world steeped in idolatry. With the possible sole exception of Luke, our Bible was written by Jewish hands, and our Lord Himself came into this world of the seed of Abraham. It is true that their national rejection of Christ robbed them for a season of their place of privilege. But we remember that through their unbelief the door of salvation was opened to us, and now it is our privilege to carry to them the Gospel which was first sent to them.

B. Dealing with the Jew.

1. *Present Christ as the Messiah.*

As that was the apostolic message to the Jews, so it must be ours. It will be well if we make the apostolic method ours also. That method was to begin with the Old Testament, taking up some of the great passages that are prophetic of Christ, and showing them fulfilled in Jesus of Nazareth. This, indeed, was our Lord's own method with His disciples as He showed them in all the Scriptures the things concerning Himself, and particularly the fact that the Christ must suffer and enter into His glory.[3]

A good course of study in preparation for this would be an examination of all the Old Testament passages used in the New Testament as referring to Christ, and shown to be fulfilled in Jesus of Nazareth.[4] One who masters these will be well armed to present the Christhood of Jesus to any thoughtful Jew. The literature of the Biblical Research Society will be found very helpful in such preparation, espe-

---

[3]Luke 24:26, 27.
[4]*See* Appendix A, page 246.

cially Dr. David Cooper's book, *Messiah, His Nature and Person.*[5]

2. Stress Need for Salvation.

But while the Messiahship of Jesus must be a central feature in our witness to Jews, we must not forget that they are sinners in need of salvation, just like others. They must be brought face to face with the fact of their personal sinnerhood. The prophets of the Old Testament have much to say about this, so the Old Testament can be used with this in view.[6]

Along with this is the fact that since the destruction of their temple, they have no divinely authorized sacrifice for sin. They have their several rituals, but, without a temple and an altar, they have nothing which answers to such a sacrifice. We know, of course, that these ancient sacrifices did not of themselves take away sin, but they were, for the time then present, the tokens of the mercy of God, and pointed to that one great sacrifice which eventually deals with sin. Here is our opportunity to point to the Lamb of God as the answer to their need and to the great lack in all their present ritual.

3. Present God's Plan for the Jews.

In some circles within the Christian Church, it is held that there is no future for the Jews. But those of us who are of the premillennial persuasion believe that the promises for the re-establishment of the Jewish nation have not been fulfilled in the church, but await the coming again of the Lord Jesus. Many a Jew has been won to Christ by being shown this plan, and the relation of this present age to that plan. One who wishes to use this approach will have to make

---

[5]David Cooper, *Messiah, His Nature and Person* (Los Angeles 65: Biblical Research Society, 4005 Verdugo Rd.).

[6]Such passages as Isa. 1:18; 53:5, 6; Jer. 2:13, 22.

a careful study of the prophetic Scriptures, and see that he knows whereof he speaks.

4. *Practical Warnings.*

There are three practical matters which I should like to mention before closing this chapter.

a) I should issue a warning to any who seek to deal with Jews not to insist on Jewish guilt in the death of Christ. It is true that they were indeed guilty, but so were the Gentiles. If the chief priests of Israel, the representatives of Jewry, handed Jesus over to Pilate with a demand that He be crucified, Pilate, representing the Roman power and the Gentile nations, treated Jesus with a complete lack of justice, and in self-interest sent Him to the cross. We ought to face the fact, also, that if Christ suffered for our sins, then we bear our own share of blame for His death. Then do not isolate the Jew as being the Christ-killer, but frankly admit that we all stand together in this responsibility.

b) Make clear the distinction between a Christian and a Gentile. The Jews have suffered much at the hands of those who professed the name of Christ but whose only excuse for calling themselves Christians was that they were not Jews. We can, therefore, point out to our Jewish friends that there is a big difference between a non-Jew and a Christian. Here is a place where we can use the Christian Scriptures, the New Testament, to show how we are under obligation as Christians to love all men, including the Jews.[7]

c) Be ready to show a Jew that in becoming a Christian he does not become any less a Jew, but that rather he becomes a true Jew. Here is also a place to use the New Testament, to point out how Peter,[8] and John,[9] and Paul[10] were

---

[7]Rom. 13:8-10; I Cor. 13.
[8]Acts 2:29; 3:13.
[9]Rev. 7:4-8.
[10]Rom. 9:1-5.

still Jews when they embraced Christ, and that their loyalty
to their nation was just as ardent as before they knew Christ.
One may then go on to indicate that a Jew is not really enjoying his privileges as a Jew[11] until he has entered into
personal relationship with the Saviour, the Messiah, the Son
of God.

As in all other departments of personal evangelism, this
also must be engaged in with much prayer.

QUESTIONS AND EXERCISES

1. What is meant by Jew-baiting? Are there any evidences of
   this in America?
2. What is a ghetto? What effect has ghetto life had on the
   Jewish character?
3. List some of the outstanding qualities of the Hebrew race,
   and give some examples of them.
4. What part has the Jewish nation played in the plan of redemption?
5. What was the apostolic method of presenting Christ to the
   Jews?
6. What great institution is lacking in Jewish worship today?
   How does the Gospel meet that lack?
7. Discuss the statement: a Jew is not a true Jew until he becomes a Christian.

---

[11]Rom. 2:28, 29.

LESSON 24

Specialties in Personal Evangelism

THE SITUATIONS in which personal evangelism comes into play are so many and varied that it would be impossible to take them all into consideration. The Christian worker will doubtless discover some particular sphere in which he can work most effectively, and make a specialty of that. In addition, he will learn to apply general principles to a variety of operations. A few of the most fruitful fields must suffice for our consideration here.

A. THE USE OF TRACTS.

We are just awakening to the value of the printed page. As evangelical Christians we have been slow to recognize this tremendous weapon, whereas we ought to have been first in the field. The fact that God gave us His revelation in the form of a Book, and said of it, "For the word of God is quick, and powerful, and sharper than any two-edged sword"[1]—that ought to have indicated to us the urgency of getting out the printed Word in every available form. Instead of this, we have played at the distribution of Christian literature, including the Word itself, while contrary forces have been scattering their evil seed everywhere. Today, with literacy at an all time high,[2] our opportunity is vastly in-

---

[1]Heb. 4:12.
[2]Russia claims an increase in literacy in 13 years from 9 per cent to 95 per cent (*Missionary Broadcaster*, November, 1955). It is well known that Japan is more literate than U.S.A. Africa is making rapid strides in this same direction.

creased, while the unbelievable activity of Communism and other false faiths in this field calls for a great forward movement by the Church of Jesus Christ.

One aspect of literary evangelism is the use of tracts, in which all of us may engage. Perhaps the craving to see immediate results tends to make us less interested in this work, for it is a form of evangelism in which we must trust for results without seeing them. For this reason every personal worker should secure a copy of Arthur Mercer's tract, *Propaganda*,[3] and read it occasionally to remind him that sowing beside all waters is indeed a profitable occupation. Here is a paragraph which describes a veritable chain reaction, and should encourage the tract distributors:

It is impossible down here to follow the course and history of every book or booklet prayerfully given, but the curtain is lifted now and again, to give us just sufficient encouragement, to show that there is a wondrous reward awaiting those who will do this work prayerfully and faithfully; and the good that one book or booklet may do, blessed by God, was never, perhaps, more powerfully illustrated than in the case of the single booklet brought in a pedlar's pack to the door of Richard Baxter's father. It was the means of the conversion of Richard Baxter, the preacher of Kidderminster. Baxter wrote the *Saints' Everlasting Rest*, which was blessed to the conversion of Philip Doddridge. Doddridge wrote the *Rise and Progress of Religion in the Soul*, which was blessed to the conversion of William Wilberforce. Wilberforce wrote his *Practical View*, which was blessed to the conversion of Legh Richmond, and Legh Richmond wrote his *Dairyman's Daughter*, which has been

---

[3]W.S.M.U. Series may be secured from Mr. Arthur Mercer, Rozel, 7, Sunnyside, Wimbledon, S.W. 19, England.

translated into more than fifty languages, and been blessed to the conversion of thousands of souls. Further, it is related that when Dr. Goodell, of the American Board, was passing through Nicomedia in 1832, having no time to stop, he left with a stranger a copy of this *Dairyman's Daughter* in the Armenian-Turkish tongue. Seventeen years afterward he visited Nicomedia, and found a church of more than 40 members, and a Protestant community of more than 200 persons. That pamphlet (to Richard Baxter's father), with God's blessing, did the work. If only the pedlar could have known what one seed that he sowed that day was going to bring forth!

1. *Be Courteous.*

Giving a tract is a fine art. Many a sincere piece of work has been lost, or has even done damage, by want of courtesy. On one occasion I was visiting a Bible school. A student, presumably taking note of the stranger, crossed the court, and without a word held out a tract for my acceptance. His countenance was set and dark, as if the act were one of stern duty which required all the determination he could muster to accomplish. I admired the young man's dogged faithfulness, but I could not but note that his manner of distributing tracts would rather repel than attract the recipients.

2. *"Introduce" the Tract.*

A tract should always be "introduced." A friendly smile and an appropriate word about the tract make all the difference. Then it ought to be *offered*, not forced. The manner of handing it, too, is important. It should be held out with the title upward and facing the party to whom it is offered. That, in brief, is the simple but necessary technique of giving a tract. It should be a perfectly natural act, betraying no embarrassment or hesitancy. Where these are in evidence, the recipient is predisposed against the literature offered. But what shall I say when handing someone a tract? Much will depend on the situation. If it can be introduced with reference to something which is in everyone's mind, so much the better. For instance, in the heat of an election one may suggest that here is something about the most important vote a man will ever cast. Where the local situation offers no help, one may at least say, "This has helped me more than anything I ever came across, and I should like to share it with you." A tract may be handed to a sales clerk with the statement, "This will tell you about the most costly thing in the world, but you may have it free." The important thing is to make it individual, not like a wholesale distribution.

3. *Avoid Wholesale Distribution.*

This brings up the question of wholesale distribution. Should one stand at a street corner "distributing" tracts? We have heard that in Japan this is successfully done, for everyone there seems hungry for something to read. In this country, however, where literature is so abundant, this method is not so good. It does not help to see the street strewn with rejected tracts. Right outside a mission, or other such center, where the distribution is done in connection with an invitation to enter, more freedom may be taken in this respect, but as a regular practice I should not encourage it. Gospel "bombs," thrown from cars on the highway, may be in a different category. Curiosity may be strong enough to induce an opening of that package and a reading of the contents. It still remains true, however, that the frank, individual offer of a piece of literature is always preferable.

4. *Use Attractive Tracts.*

There is no excuse today for offering people cheap-looking, unattractive tracts. Since modern printing techniques

were applied to this department of literature, it is easy to
secure tracts as attractive as anything in the secular world,
while at the same time carrying the greatest message in
the world. But a tract is more than good stock and good
printing. There is as much technique in writing a tract as
in printing or giving one. A tract is like an editorial. It must
command attention. It must say what it has to say briefly
and clearly. It must not be sermonic. Its approach must be
psychologically sound even as its message must be doctrinal-
ly sound. For instance, I saw a tract recently which began,
"I have a question to ask you." One's immediate reaction
to that is, "Who are you to ask me questions?" People shy
away from questioning. A much better approach would be:
"I have something most valuable to share with you." The
"question" may come later. There needs to be discrimina-
tion in the matter of what tracts to use as well as care in the
manner of using them.

5. *Back Up Distribution with Prayer.*

Like all other evangelistic activities, this giving of tracts
must be accompanied by much prayer—prayer for guidance
in giving them, and prayer for the prosperity of the Word in
opening men's hearts to Christ. A Gospel card in the purse
of "Sister Abigail," backed by prayer, was the means of the
conversion of the pickpocket who stole her purse, and of his
two companions, all three of them becoming earnest soul-
winners.[4]

B. HOSPITAL VISITATION.

An excellent sphere for personal work is the hospital.
Chaplain Alvin Bray, of Cook County Hospital in Chicago,
calls it a "natural" for evangelism. In sickness one is more

---

[4]Clara S. Feidler, *Sister Abigail* (Buffalo: Sword and Shield Book Store),
pp. 187-195.

likely to be concerned about his relation to God and his soul's welfare. But this must not be depended on too much. The sick are more easily disturbed and annoyed, and the approach to them must be with care.

1. Get Backing of Organization.

It is usually better to have the backing of a recognized organization if one wishes to engage in hospital visitation. Free lances are not generally welcome, but are regarded as intruders. Hospital authorities, however, will give the needed permissions to one who comes with proper sanctions. To undertake this work without permission will not only be met with resistance, but will make it more difficult for others to receive authorization.

2. Respect Wishes of Patient.

A hospital visitor must offer himself to a patient rather than impose himself upon the sick person. A disinclination to receive the visitor is not necessarily enmity or bad disposition, and when one respects the manifest wishes of the patient, it is likely to make him more acceptable the next time. To insist on visiting where one is not wanted will only prejudice the whole case.

3. Be Brief, Cheerful, and Quiet.

Three words should ever be remembered by those working with sick people—brevity, cheerfulness, and quietness. One of the principal "gripes" of hospital authorities is the interminable, loud visitor who brings to the patient all sorts of doleful gossip. Our message can be given in very few words. It is a glad message. It is a message of peace. Therefore there is no excuse for our failing to be brief, cheerful, and quiet. Of course, if the sick person wants to unburden his heart, one should listen; but even then the patient may have to be controlled, and not be allowed to jeopardize his re-

covery by too much emotion or exertion. Much wisdom is
needed here.

The practice of distributing tracts from bed to bed, laying
them on the beds or side-tables without permission of the
patients, is of doubtful ethics. A tract should be offered, and
left only by consent of the party.

4. *Choose Tracts Wisely.*

Here is a case where the choice of tracts is of the utmost
importance. Screaming titles have no place here, and the
message ought to be the positive truth of the Gospel, strongly flavored with the love and tenderness of God.

Some zealous but unwise souls, while ostensibly speaking
to one person, have tried preaching to the whole ward, raising the voice so that all could hear. To say the least, this is
bad taste. It is embarrassing to the individual supposedly
addressed, and disturbing and offensive to all. Speak quietly, giving all your thought and attention to the one person.
If the patient in the next bed has keen ears, and overhears
what you are saying, your very quietness and thoughtfulness may dispose him to accept your Saviour.

5. *Co-operate with Staff.*

We admit that the spiritual welfare of the patient is of
primary importance, and in some hospitals that is acknowledged. I remember hearing a superintendent, at a capping
ceremony, insisting that the nurses must remember their
responsibility to the souls as well as the bodies of the patients. That was a Christian hospital! At the same time,
these people have brought their sick bodies there for treatment, and the nurses are under orders to carry out a certain
program of treatment for each patient. We must yield
place to the nurse in her round of duties, and not insist on
the priority of our spiritual ministry. We shall promote our

spiritual ministry more by co-operation and thoughtfulness than by any superior attitude.

C. THE OPEN-AIR MEETING.

The open-air meeting offers good opportunities for personal work. There is, of course, the corporate witness of the group organizing the open-air service, but the personal worker is a vital factor in that effort.

1. *Invite into Circle.*

The first effort of the personal worker will be to invite any who stop and listen to come into the circle, perhaps by offering to share a hymnbook during singing. If the invitation is accepted, you have an interested listener. He may not wish to stay all the time, so when he turns to go, the alert worker will step a few paces from the circle with him, express pleasure in having met him, and offer him an attractive tract, while at the same time inquiring very kindly whether he knows the Saviour of whom he has been hearing. This situation would generally call for the direct approach, the subject already having been broached in the public meeting. The friend's response would determine whether the matter should be pursued further, or whether one should be satisfied with extending a gracious invitation to come again. There may also be an invitation to attend services in the church holding the open-air meetings, especially if it becomes known that the visitor has no regular church connection. Another result of such a conversation may be an arrangement to meet and talk matters over. This, of course, must only be between man and man, or between woman and woman. In this situation, no arrangement to meet again should be made between members of the opposite sexes.

2. *Make Necessary Arrangements.*

While the arrangements of an open-air meeting do not come within the compass of personal evangelism, I should like to offer a few suggestions in this regard.

a) Be sure to have the necessary permission from the police department, and the good will of the policeman on the beat where the meeting is to be held.

b) Make careful choice of the place of meeting. Where a side street enters a main thoroughfare is a good location, especially if there is considerable pedestrian traffic on the main street. A park frequented by people with time on their hands is an excellent place. Cross-streets that are particularly noisy, with the screech of streetcars or buses turning the corner, create a definite handicap. A spot should be chosen where the light is good, and where sound carries.

c) If the meeting is held just outside a store, make the acquaintance and seek the good will of the merchant. The services are not likely to be held during store hours, but even so, a gracious attitude will always do good. In Sault Ste Marie, Ontario, the proprietor of the large hardware store on whose broad walk we held our meetings fixed up a powerful overhanging light for us and arranged to have it switched on every Sunday evening.

d) Secure proper equipment: a portable organ, a few trumpets or accordions, a small collapsible platform, small hymnbooks or hymn sheets with a good selection of the best known hymns and Gospel songs, and a public address system if permitted and available.

e) Identify yourselves, by means of a banner or some such device. There are so many vendors of strange doctrines conducting open-air meetings, and introducing their fallacies surreptitiously, that it is good for God's people to make themselves known. If several churches will combine, it will be so much more effective.

f) Have a planned program. Do not depend on the impulse of the moment, or just hope that some talent will be present. Prepare your service as carefully as you do an indoor service, and see that it keeps going. Do not call for testimonies "from the floor," but have them arranged ahead of time.

g) Keep every item brief: no long solos, no long prayers, no long testimonies, no long sermons. And let there be variety, not only within each service, but from meeting to meeting. Here is a place for ingenuity.

h) Have spotters on the job, ready to act as we indicated earlier in this lesson.

In open-air work one must be prepared for hecklers. In this case it is absolutely necessary to keep one's temper. To show anger is to go down in defeat. At the same time, a sharp answer, with a real touch of humor, will not only silence the heckler, but will secure the interest of the hearers. Dad Hall, "Bishop of Wall Street," was once interrupted in an open-air meeting with the question, "Will you please tell me where the Devil is?" Quick as an arrow he replied, "Just now he is standing right in front of me disturbing this meeting."[5] Perhaps that was a bit sharp, but it secured all ears for the preacher.

D. THE INQUIRY ROOM.

The inquiry room is a place prepared for the personal worker. Whether it be the old-fashioned "mourner's bench" or a counseling room, there is the same work to be done. In large campaigns, like those of Billy Graham, this phase

---

[5]Sara C. Palmer, *Dad Hall* (Chicago 10: Moody Press), p. 103.

of the work requires elaborate organization and the most careful supervision. But even in smaller evangelistic undertakings, where only one church is involved, there should be no taking things for granted.

1. *Personal Workers To Be Instructed.*

The personal workers ought to be instructed and trained ahead of time, and only those allowed to act who are willing to follow the rules. The work of the inquiry room should be supervised, even if the only one available to do so is the pastor or the evangelist.

Male personal workers should always deal with men, and women with women. Even in the case of children, it is good to follow this rule.

The personal worker must avoid any suggestion of lecturing or preaching. In one of my early campaigns I went into the inquiry room to find an earnest young man standing in front of a frightened boy, lecturing him as a sergeant would lecture a new recruit! Sit down beside the inquirer and act like a friend.

a) The first necessity is to discover the exact state of the inquirer. A physician does not prescribe before diagnosing the disease. Now, while the physician can look at the throat and take the pulse, and listen to the heart-beat, we must largely diagnose from what the inquirer himself says. The counselor can begin by asking, very kindly, "What is the burden on your heart?" The answer will give a fairly clear indication of the particular problem. If there is an immediate confession of sin and expressed desire for forgiveness, there is little difficulty. If, however, the answer reveals some remnants of self-righteousness, some intellectual doubts, the counselor must act with great wisdom, which may be obtained for the asking.[6] (The lessons on special cases deal with the problems likely to be met with here.)

b) It is important that the personal worker use his Bible. Appropriate verses should be used, and usually the inquirer himself should be asked to read them. Eye-gate then cooperates with ear-gate, and hearing the truth uttered *by his own voice* is a valuable aid. A wise counselor will not use too many verses, which may become confusing. It is much better to stick to one verse (provided it is an appropriate one for the situation!) until, by repeated usage, its truth begins to take hold. It will be found that one verse lends itself to a good many emphases.

c) When the counselor discerns that the inquirer is ready for decision, it is a wholesome practice to suggest kneeling together, so long as there is no physical disability. Frequently it will be found that the heart will bend with the knees. Moreover, most people mentally relate kneeling and praying, so the first prayer of penitence and trust becomes easier in the kneeling posture. In many cases, the worker will have to assist the deciding soul to formulate that first prayer, and the one used in so many rescue missions can well be borrowed: "God be merciful to me a sinner, and save me, for Jesus' sake. Amen."

d) Never tell a young convert that he is saved. Let the Holy Spirit tell him, and let him tell you. And be sure that the ground of his trust is the perfect work of Christ, and that his certainty is based on the sure Word of God. That is of supreme importance.

2. *Follow-up Work To Be Started.*

When the inquirer is satisfied that he is now a child of God, such follow-up as the situation calls for should imme-

---

[6]James 1:5.

diately begin. The name and address should be secured, along with such other information as is called for on the decision card which may be in use. When possible, the young convert should be introduced to the pastor or the evangelist, who will give words of encouragement and counsel. A church ought to provide well-selected literature for new Christians, to help them as they take their first steps.[7] They should also be encouraged to undertake a course of Bible memorization, such as that prepared by The Navigators.[8]

3. *Rescue Mission Problems.*

The inquiry room of a rescue mission presents situations rather different from those met with elsewhere. Often enough the inquirers are in various stages of drunkenness, or more or less under the influence of drugs. Sometimes one will find his way into the inquiry room and begin to create a disturbance. It is always better to allow one of the regular staff of the mission to handle such situations. Mission superintendents learn when to administer the "rod," and can usually quiet the most obstreperous. The visiting worker should not interfere in such cases.

Mr. Harry Saulnier, superintendent of the Pacific Garden Mission in Chicago, encourages his workers to get inquirers on their knees immediately they begin dealing with them in the inquiry room. The reason for this is that men and women in the condition which usually prevails there can have their attention so easily diverted from the matter on hand. If they sit facing the room, everything that takes place distracts them. But if they are kneeling with nothing before them but the back of a chair and the wall, they can be more easily held to the point. A second suggestion from this ex-

---

[7]I heartily recommend Stephen Olford's pamphlets, *Becoming a Child of God, Becoming a Man of God, and Becoming a Servant of God* (London, W.1, England: C.S.S.M. 5, Wigmore Street).
[8]The Navigators, Colorado Springs, Colorado.

perienced servant of God is that the worker have the inquirer actually put his finger on the passage of Scripture being used. And here it is more important than ever to stick to one verse, having it repeated again and again.

Some may question the advisability of dealing with a "drunk." By all means, yes. Many a man has been converted in a state of drunkenness, and conversion sobered him more quickly than the blackest coffee ever could. Remember that the Holy Spirit is working along with us, and He is able to penetrate the darkness and make the light shine.

E. INSTITUTIONS.

There are many other opportunities offered for personal evangelism, such as in jails, charitable institutions, and service centers, all calling for their own special adaptations of the same general principles.

Perhaps jails are among the most difficult fields of evangelism. Strange as it may seem, criminals are among the most self-righteous people one can find. They want to tell you what good fellows they are, and how they were framed, and so on. Some, for sure, are tough, but these will probably refuse to speak to a Christian worker. They are cynical and superior. Yet there are always some who feel the humiliation of their situation, and are ready to listen. In dealing with these men, we must avoid conveying the impression that they are outcasts, or that we are in a different class from them. Certainly we must not rub in the fact that they .are criminals. Rather we must show them from the Word of God that they are *sinners*, just as we are. They must be taught to relate all they have done to God,[9] and shown God's provision for making them new creatures. If they show true

---

[9] Ps. 51:4.

repentance, we must seek to have them dwell on God's free and full pardon rather than on their past. Our purpose in dealing with all sinners is to bring them to the Saviour, so that they may know that their past is cast into the depths of the sea,[10] and they are beginning a new life.

I should like to close this lesson with a word of counsel which Sister Eva, of Friedenshort, gave to her workers with respect to work in jails. "Now a piece of advice! Do not allow anyone to tell you *any more* than is absolutely necessary for confession and unburdening of the soul. There are unclean minds who think it necessary to tell about hateful things with all possible detail. Do not allow that. It is enough that you should be told what is in question; all fuller description of what happened is to be avoided as far as possible. If they are not able to express themselves and yet desire to confess, ask simply: 'Against what commandment have you sinned?' That is enough. How it happened, by what means and so on—in most cases that has nothing to do with the matter, and one should dwell as little as possible on the *sin,* but quickly go with the burden to the Saviour of sinners. But you must require from the souls whom you serve a decided break with the sin. A confession should be a renunciation. One who confesses and lives on in sin asks in vain for mercy. One cannot warn enough against that."[11]

Whatever be the particular sphere in which we are privileged to engage in a witness for our Lord Jesus Christ, let us keep in remembrance the words of the apostle Paul: "Now then we are ambassadors for Christ, as though God did beseech you by us: we pray you in Christ's stead, be ye

[10]Mic. 7:19.
[11]Sister Annie, *Sister Eva of Friedenshort* (London: Hodder and Stoughton), p. 220.

reconciled to God."[12] Faithfulness, earnestness, and urgency, coupled with the wisdom which God gives, must characterize all our labors.

Let a few Scottish lines, whose author I unfortunately do not know, end our study but urge our endeavors.

> The time for sawin' seed, it is wearin', wearin' dune;
> An' the time for winnin' souls will be ower verra sune:
> Then let us a' be active, if a fruitfu' sheaf we'd bring
> To adorn the royal table in the palace o' the King.

QUESTIONS AND EXERCISES

1. Write a brief paper on the advance of literacy in Russia, Africa, and Japan, as this affects the work of the Gospel.
2. What is meant by "introducing" a tract? Give examples.
3. What three words would constitute the motto of all who engage in hospital visitation? Explain.
4. Write a list of the items you would want to take care of in arranging an open-air meeting.
5. Here is a suggestion for a research paper: *The History of the Inquiry Room.*
6. What special precautions should be taken in the inquiry room of a rescue mission?
7. Write briefly on the peculiar difficulties encountered in jail work.

---

[12]II Cor. 5:20.

Appendix

A list of Old Testament passages referred to in the New Testament as being fulfilled in Christ in the days of His humiliation.

New Testament	*Old Testament*
Matthew 1:23	Isaiah 7:14
Matthew 2:6	Micah 5:2
Matthew 2:15	Hosea 11:1
Matthew 2:18	Jeremiah 31:15
Matthew 4:15	Isaiah 9:1
Matthew 8:17	Isaiah 53:4
Matthew 12:18	Isaiah 41:8; 42:1-4
Matthew 13:35	Psalm 78:2
Matthew 21:5	Zechariah 9:9
Matthew 21:9	Psalm 118:26
Matthew 21:42	Psalm 118:22
Matthew 22:44	Psalm 110:1
Matthew 26:31	Zechariah 8:7
Matthew 27:9	Zechariah 11:13
Matthew 27:35	Psalm 22:18
Mark 11:9	Psalm 118:26
Mark 12:10	Psalm 118:22
Mark 12:36	Psalm 110:1
Mark 14:27	Zechariah 13:7
Mark 15:34	Psalm 22:1
Luke 4:18	Isaiah 61:1

New Testament	Old Testament
Luke 19:38	Psalm 118:26
Luke 20:17	Psalm 118:22
Luke 20:42	Psalm 110:1
Luke 22:37	Isaiah 53:12
John 2:17	Psalm 69:9
John 7:42	Psalm 89:3, 4
John 12:13	Psalm 118:26
John 12:15	Zechariah 9:9
John 12:38	Isaiah 53:1
John 13:18	Psalm 41:9
John 15:25	Psalms 35:19; 69:4
John 19:24	Psalm 22:18
John 19:28	Psalm 69:21
John 19:36	Exodus 12:46; Numbers 9:12; Psalm 34:20
John 19:37	Zechariah 12:10
Acts 2:25-31	Psalms 16:8-11; 132:11
Acts 2:34	Psalm 110:1
Acts 3:22, 23	Deuteronomy 18:15, 18; Leviticus 23:29
Acts 4:11	Psalm 118:22
Acts 4:25	Psalm 2:1, 2
Acts 8:32	Isaiah 53:7
Acts 13:33, 34	Psalms 2:7; 16:10; Isaiah 55:3
Romans 4:25	Isaiah 53:12
Romans 9:33	Isaiah 28:16 (LXX)
Romans 15:3	Psalm 69:9
Galatians 3:13	Deuteronomy 21:23
Galatians 3:16	Genesis 12:7; 13:15; 17:7; 22:18; 24:7
Hebrews 1:5	Psalm 2:7; II Samuel 7:14
Hebrews 2:6-9	Psalm 8:4

New Testament	Old Testament
Hebrews 2:16	Isaiah 41:8
Hebrews 2:12	Psalm 22:22
Hebrews 5:5	Psalm 2:7
Hebrews 8:8-13	Jeremiah 31:31-34
Hebrews 10:5-10	Psalm 40:6-8
I Peter 2:6	Isaiah 28:16
I Peter 2:7, 8	Psalm 118:22; Isaiah 8:14
I Peter 2:22	Isaiah 53:9
I Peter 2:24	Isaiah 53:5, 12

Bibliography

Works Referred to in Text

Annie, Sister. *Sister Eva of Friedenshort.* London: Hodder and Stoughton.

Begbie, Harold. *Twice-Born Men.* Westwood, N.J.: Revell.

Bonar, Andrew A. *Memoir and Remains of R. M. M'Cheyne.* Edinburgh: Oliphant, Anderson, and Ferrier.

Bonar, Horatius. *Words to the Winner of Souls.* New York: American Tract Society.

Bready, J. Wesley. *England Before and After Wesley.* London: Hodder and Stoughton.

————. *This Freedom Whence?* New York: American Tract Society.

Cartwright, Lin. *Evangelism for Today.* St. Louis: The Bethany Press.

Chafer, L. S. *True Evangelism.* Findlay, Ohio: Dunham Co.

Clow, W. M. *The Cross in Christian Experience.*

Cooper, David. *Messiah, His Nature and Person.* Los Angeles: Biblical Research Society.

Denny, James. *The Christian Doctrine of Reconciliation.* London: Hodder and Stoughton.

Edwards, Jonathan. *The Life and Diary of David Brainerd.* Chicago: Moody Press.

Feidler, Clara S. *Sister Abigail.* Buffalo: Sword and Shield Book Store.

Fletcher, Lionel B. *The Effective Evangelist.*

Goodman, Paul. *A History of the Jews.* Cleveland: World Publishing Co.

Graham, Billy. *Peace with God.* Westwood, N.J.: Revell.

Judson, Edward. *The Life of Adoniram Judson.* New York: Anson Randolph & Co.

Langston, E. L. *Bishop Taylor Smith.* London: Marshall, Morgan and Scott.

Macaulay, J. C. *The Bible and the Roman Church.* Chicago: Moody Press.

Magnus, Lady. *Outlines of Jewish History.* Philadelphia: Jewish Publication Co. of America.

Mathieson, Alfred. *Hebich of India.* Scotland: John Ritchie, Ltd.

Palmer, Sara C. *Dad Hall.* Chicago: Moody Press.

Roth, Cecil. *A Bird's-eye View of Jewish History.* Cincinnati 2: Riverdale Press.

Smith, Gypsy. *Gypsy Smith, His Life and Work.* London: Law.

Smith, Oswald J. *The Consuming Fire.* Grand Rapids: Zondervan Publishing House.

Spurgeon, C. H. *The Soul-Winner.* Westwood, N.J.: Revell.

Torrey, R. A. *Soul-Winning Sermons.* Westwood, N.J.: Revell.

Trumbull, H. Clay. *Individual Work for Individuals.* New York: Association Press.

Trumbull, Charles G. *Taking Men Alive.* New York: Association Press.

VanBaalen, J. K. *The Chaos of Cults.* Grand Rapids: Eerdmans Publishing Co.

Vassar, Thomas E. *Uncle John Vassar.* New York: American Tract Society.

Walker, F. D., *William Carey.* Chicago: Moody Press.

Additional Works

Bibliography listed here is only representative; no attempt is made at completeness. Some publications listed are out of print and can be secured second-hand.

Benson, C. H. *The Church at Work.*

Chapman, J. Wilbur. *The Personal Touch.* Westwood, N.J.: Revell.

———. *The Problem of the Work.* London: Hodder and Stoughton.

Conant, J. E. *Every Member Evangelism.* Philadelphia: The Sunday School Times.

Evans, William. *Personal Soul-Winning.* Chicago: Moody Press.

Goodell, Charles L. *Motives and Methods of Modern Evangelism.* Westwood, N.J.: Revell.

———. *Pastoral and Personal Evangelism.* Westwood, N.J.: Revell.

———. *Pastor and Evangelist.*

Goodman, Frederic S. *Evangelism Through Bible Study.* Philadelphia: Sunday School Times.

Hallenback, Edwin. *The Passion for Souls.* Chicago: Winona Publishing Co.

Harrison, Eugene Myers and Walter L. Wilson. *How To Win Souls.* Chicago: Scripture Press.

Henson, L. L. *The Lost Secret Recovered.* Philadelphia: Winston.

Hicks, Jos. P. *Ten Lessons in Personal Evangelism.*

Jowett, J. H. *The Passion for Souls.* New York: Grossett and Dunlap.

Kemp, Joseph. *The Soul-Winner and Soul-Winning.*

Kernahan, A. Earl. *Visitation Evangelism.* Westwood, N.J.: Revell.

Lamb, M. T. *Won by One.* England: Signs Publications.

Leete, F. D. *Every-Day Evangelism.* Cincinnati: Jennings and Graham.

Mabie, H. C. *Methods in Soul-Winning.* Westwood, N.J.: Revell.

Mahood, J. W. *The Art of Soul-Winning.* Cincinnati: Jennings and Pye.

Massee, J. C. *Evangelism in the Local Church.* Philadelphia: Judson Press.

Morgan, G. Campbell. *Evangelism.* Westwood, N.J.: Revell.

Mott, John R. *The Larger Evangelism.* New York: Abingdon-Cokesbury.

Odell, Jack. *Not the Righteous.* Westwood, N.J.: Revell.

Oliver, G. F. *Soul-Winners' Secrets.* New York: Jennings and Pye.

Pierson, A. T. *Evangelistic Work in Principle and Practice.* New York: Baker and Taylor.

Pratt, D. M. *The Master's Method of Winning Men.* Westwood, N.J.: Revell.

Rice, John R. *The Soul-Winner's Fire.* Chicago: Moody Press.

Scarborough, L. R. *How Jesus Won Men.*

————. *With Christ After the Lost.* Nashville: Sunday School Board, Southern Baptist Convention.

Soltau, George. *Personal Work for Christ.* London: Roberts.

Stone, John Timothy. *Recruiting for Christ.* Westwood, N.J.: Revell.

————. *Winning Men.* Westwood, N.J.: Revell.

Torrey, R. A. *How To Work for Christ.* London: James Nisbet and Co. Ltd.

Index